CW00343817

CAME THE DAWN

50 Years an Army Officer

INVICTA
ROYAL
WEST
KENT

CAME THE DAWN

50 Years an Army Officer

Brigadier Paul Crook
CBE DSO MA

SPELLMOUNT LTD
Tunbridge Wells

In the Spellmount Military list:
The Territorial Battalions – A pictorial history
The Yeomanry Regiments – A pictorial history
Over the Rhine – The Last Days of War in Europe
History of the Cambridge University OTC
Yeoman Service
The Fighting Troops of the Austro-Hungarian Army
Intelligence Officer in the Peninsula
The Scottish Regiments – A pictorial history
The Royal Marines – A pictorial history
The Royal Tank Regiment – A pictorial history
The Irish Regiments – A pictorial history
British Sieges of the Peninsular War
Victoria's Victories
Rorke's Drift
Napoleon's Military Machine
Heaven and Hell – German paratroop war diary
Wellington's Military Machine

In the Nautical list:
Sea of Memories
Evolution of Engineering in the Royal Navy Vol 1 1827-1939

In the Aviation list:
Diary of a Bomb Aimer

First published in the UK in 1989 by
Spellmount Ltd, 12 Dene Way, Speldhurst,
Tunbridge Wells, Kent TN3 0NX

ISBN 0-946771-21-9

British Library Cataloguing in Publication Data
Crook, Paul E.
Came the dawn: 50 years an army officer
1. Great Britain. *Army* – Biographies
I. Title
355'.0092'4

Typeset by Vitaset, Paddock Wood, Kent
Design & Artwork Preparation by Projects Thirty-Seven Limited, Paddock Wood. Kent
Printed in Great Britain by The Ipswich Book Co Ltd, Ipswich, Suffolk

Contents

List of Illustrations

Foreword

by General Sir Geoffrey Howlett, KBE MC
Commander-in-Chief, Allied Forces Northern Europe
1986-89 Colonel Commandant The Parachute Regiment

This *potpourri* of happenings actually all befell one man, an infantry officer Paul Crook in the period spanning the immediate pre-war years, the 39-45 War and its aftermath when the British Army played such a conspicuous part in the withdrawal from Empire. I know that I could not promise such a time to a young man joining today but then even when Paul Crook joined not everyone had his sense of fun or his ability to make the most of his travels and adventures.

His love of cricket and sport may have been reasonably conventional, his enthusiasm for jazz certainly was not. His soldiering took him from Palestine to Parachuting, from Java to Jamaica, from the Gold Coast to Golf, America to Aden, with India, Normandy, Suez, Cyprus and Malaya thrown in. He taught at the Staff College, sang at Hatchetts, represented Jamaica at President Kennedy's funeral and worked with Orde Wingate and Edwina Mountbatten. He also commanded the only British parachute battalion to have jumped operationally since 1945, at Port Said in 1956.

I have been lucky enough to have served under him twice and to have shared a little of the fun he reflected around him. I have played cricket and hockey with him, I have heard him sing and I have drunk considerable quantities of his hospitality in many lands! More importantly he was both my first Company Commander and my first Commanding Officer when I joined the Parachute Regiment. His influence on me was great – not by formal teaching but by the well-tried method of 'Look and Learn'. He was tolerant of youth and its mistakes – he encouraged you to have ideas and to use them and, above all, he backed and supported you when you got it wrong. You did not get it wrong twice though!

These tales are not military or political history, but they do tell a story of how much the soldier has had to bail a Nation's politicians out of the mire throughout the world. I doubt that Paul Crook really regrets many of those Dawns though.

For BETTY
without whom this book would not have been written

Preface

Arma virumque cano. (I sing of arms and men). – Virgil

'You ought to write a book about it.'

Those words were not infrequently said to me by friends and colleagues. The 'it' is the story of the Suez affair in 1956. The thinking behind this is that I was there both in the air and on the ground and knew what actually happened in contrast to the many accounts concocted by people who were not. But my part was limited to the airborne assault, fighting for two days and occupying Port Said for a week. I can give a factual account of this. But I know little of the intrigues and political manoeuvring which went on behind the scenes. Too many people have written about this already.

But if their accounts of the political background are as inaccurate as their accounts of the actual military activities, then they are very far from the truth. They illustrate the aphorism that contemporary history is 'his story about something that didn't happen by someone who wasn't there'.

So I steadfastly refused to write a book about 'it' on the grounds that what I had to say would only fill a chapter. In the event it has become four chapters in this book which came to be written for two good reasons, the weather and my wife.

During a long period of snow and ice when it was impossible to play golf, my wife became fed up with my hanging around at home like a caged tiger and said, 'Now is the time to start on that book. There are boxes of material in the attic which we have been carting around and storing for years, and it's time you did something with them.'

So reluctantly I acquiesced and, as even I cannot read my own writing, acquired a word processor.

This is the story of one soldier's life and experiences spanning fifty years of commissioned service. It is a tale told from memory of certain events as I saw them. You will not find deep philosophical musings on how these events influenced history but just how they affected me.

Recollections are funny things inevitably blurred and tinged with wishful thinking. Efforts have been made to check the facts but no guarantees can be given as to complete accuracy. Mistakes there must be but quite innocent and I apologise to anyone who may be disturbed by them.

When looking back there are problems over place names and ranks which have changed with time. As a general rule I have given the rank and title held by people at the period described and the same with the names of countries and towns.

My grateful thanks are due to General Sir Geoffrey Howlett for advice and the Foreword, to Mrs Helen Sears for invaluable secretarial assistance, and to Cyril Middleton for help with the photos.

1
Early Days

And Thomas here's my best respects to you – Rudyard Kipling.

Dawn is breaking over Karachi. A dawn which some fifty years ago found me in the front of an army truck bumping through the city, surprised to see some of its inhabitants wrapped in blankets shivering in doorways of shuttered shops. Surprised because to shiver at any time in such a climate was an unexpected phenomenon to a new arrival in the tropics. But shiver they did. Meanwhile we made our way to army ranges on the edge of the Sind Desert, grateful for a period of comparative cool in which to indulge in various shooting activities before succumbing to the heat of the day.

To go back to the beginning: I was born some twenty-one years before this and educated at Uppingham School and Emmanuel College, Cambridge, where I gained a Bachelor of Arts degree. I had read Classics and Law, a promising background for a budding barrack-room lawyer; I always wanted an active outdoor sporting life and chose the Army as a career.

In 1936 I was commissioned into the Queen's Own Royal West Kent Regiment and posted to the 2nd Battalion stationed at Shorncliffe near Folkestone, Kent. Whilst with the Cambridge Officers' Training Corps I had carried out an attachment to the Battalion, and was greeted with some enthusiasm by the young subalterns, my contemporaries, as being the lowest of the low, junior to all of them. However, my Cambridge degree earned me an ante-date of twenty-one months on being commissioned as a regular officer and so, overnight, I became senior to eleven Second Lieutenants. This was in the days before automatic promotion by time to Captain and Major, and some unfortunates had been known to wait as long as twenty years before filling a vacancy for Captain in dead man's shoes. Thus, anyone jumping the queue was hardly likely to be greeted with wild enthusiasm.

Such was the oddity of the situation that shortly after my arrival I found myself in acting command of a Company in the absence of their Captain on 'extended hunting leave'. The Company Sergeant Major competently ran the Company and all went well.

At this time I was greatly enamoured of and affianced to a very lovely lady who worked in Fleet Street. She was able to visit from time to time and then dawn activities consisted of frantic dashes from an hotel in Sandgate, up the steep hill to the barracks in Shorncliffe above, in time to be properly dressed, puttees and all, for the early morning parade.

The role of the Home Battalion was to train and supply reinforcements for the Overseas Battalion. And so a Second Lieutenant of some paper service if not practical experience (me) was due to go on this six year tour of service abroad, leaving his loved ones behind, and a very sad parting ensued.

The War Office Movements Branch moved in its mysterious way and sent a batch of junior officers out to India on a luxury liner, while much senior officers were detailed to bring out drafts of troops on elderly, primitive troop ships. Among the more congenial of my companions were Tony Innes joining the Lincolns, and Dickie Lonsdale joining the Leicesters. There was a decent band on board and I was able to enjoy myself at times singing with it.

Perhaps I should digress here and explain this singing with bands business. Coming from a musical family I was brought up to enjoy all forms of music but I found that I had a genuine very deep love of jazz. Jazz in the late thirties was in one of its very best periods and the 'swing' era was developing in the USA. But there was then very little true jazz in the United Kingdom and such as there was I sought out. I was one of a welcoming party for Louis Armstrong when he came to Cambridge, and spent an hilarious session with Fats Waller in his dressing room between performances at the London Palladium. I was to meet up with Louis again in America. The most important item in my kit was a portable gramophone which I took everywhere with me. I gave as much thought to the compilation of the dozen or so records I could take with it as people do for their programme 'Desert Island Discs'. Duke Ellington's *Mood Indigo* was always number one.

I seemed to have a flair for rhythmic vocalising and modelled myself on the Bing Crosby of those days, the Mills Brothers, the Boswell Sisters, and of course Louis Armstrong, pinching phrases from each of them. The result was apparently quite pleasing, with a genuine feel for swing. My friends at Cambridge said I should take it more seriously and bullied me into entering for a crooning competition. To my surprise I won it with a rendering of a little ditty called *Dinah*.

And now back to Karachi . . .

The Battalion should have been stationed in Quetta but there had been a terrible earthquake there and the barracks had been destroyed. We were accommodated in a temporary camp just outside Karachi by the dusty racecourse. It was fairly primitive and many of us were in tents, not at all comfortable by peacetime standards. There were no married quarters and the families had been sent home, so we all lived together senior and junior officers, young and old soldiers alike. The Battalion had been stationed in India for eighteen years and some of the soldiers had served with it throughout. Indeed one of them, Pte 'Nobby' Esplin had been in India continuously for thirty-four years. He became a celebrity on his return to the UK in 1938 and was featured in 'In Town Tonight'. Meanwhile he was a celebrity in his own right in the Battalion. In his capacity as a Company Storeman he could produce virtually anything from a cap badge to a Lewis gun if treated right. This was invaluable to a young officer who might have lost some military item – a terrible crime in those days. He was respected by all, from the Commanding Officer downwards. Nothing was allowed to interfere with his routine which included a pint of beer on the stroke of twelve noon. Once when bidden to attend the CO's Orders to give evidence at midday, he respectfully declined saying: 'The CO knows full well that I have business in the canteen at that time.'

Military activities started with parades very early in the morning, if not quite at dawn, though there were some vivid dawns in the Sind Desert where we went for manoeuvres. A considerable amount of footwork was required of the infantry soldier in those far off days when motor transport was still a rarity. A piece of badinage used to cheer me up as I trudged wearily along with my Platoon. First soldier: 'Join the Army and see the world.' Second soldier: 'Yes and join the West Kents and walk effing round it.' This helped to keep us going to the next halt.

Normally, after a siesta there was much sporting activity. During the time in India we had developed some very good games players and especially an outstanding hockey team capable of giving anyone a game, including the Indian Olympic Team, who only just beat us in a practice match. I had difficulty in getting into the side. Cricket was a little easier as the hard but true matting wickets suited me and I managed to make the European team against the other Communities.

That year Lord Tennyson brought a strong MCC side to India, including Joe Hardstaff, then England's leading batsman. They came to play the locals and to our amusement and surprise could not bowl them out any more easily than we could. But shocks were in store when it came to the MCC's turn to bat and they were soon in trouble with the loss of two quick wickets. Batting at number four, Joe Hardstaff started confidently with a beautiful boundary. He was then at the non-striker's end whilst the Hindu fast bowler started on his long run-up. Joe backed up a little enthusiastically and was out of his ground when the Hindu bowler stopped at the wicket, knocked off the bails with a ball, and appealed. Sadly of course he was technically out and the unfortunate umpire had to uphold the appeal. As he walked out the jeers and boos for the bowler and umpire grew to a crescendo; soon fighting broke out between the Muslim and Hindu elements among the spectators and a stand collapsed. The West Kent soldiers, who had long been starved of class English batting, were not best pleased either. Fireworks were thrown at the Hindu bowler and it was some time before order was restored and he could finish his over. A rare happening in the first-class cricket scene in those days but one that was to become only too common. After all this, wickets fell at regular intervals and things began to look bad for the English team. However, there was still the gallant Lord Tennyson to bat. Marching purposefully from our Regimental tent where he had been partaking of strong liquor he proceeded to strike the hitherto successful bowling all over and out of the ground with gay abandon. He soon reached an astonishing and invaluable century and the honour of the British Raj was upheld.

Cricket is one of my main loves and, as I have indicated, jazz another. There was not much of the latter in Karachi except at the Railway Institute Club for Anglo-Indians about a mile away from the camp, which was more or less out of bounds to Pukka Sahibs. Some of the ladies were very attractive but I was impervious to their charms, being strictly faithful to my fiancée in UK. But the music did attract and during a rare visit I found myself at the microphone giving it all I had got, in a jam session with the band. Most of those present seemed to enjoy it but unfortunately the sentiment was not shared by all my listeners. The performance was out of doors and on a still, tropical night the sound travelled only too distinctly across the open, sandy space to the camp. There it both infuriated and kept awake a very senior officer who did not appreciate it at all. The next morning he was very cross and suspicious but never directly associated it with me. This was just as well.

One Sunday I was Orderly Officer and so confined to barracks, unlike the rest of my brother officers. I ate a hearty breakfast which included a treat, some cold ham. I inspected the barracks as usual with the Orderly Sergeant; on reaching the Sergeants' Mess for refreshment, I was suddenly taken ill and very sick. At first the beer was blamed but I was soon much too ill to know or care what it was and was carted off to hospital. There I was joined at intervals by my colleagues from various places in Karachi such as the sailing, swimming and tennis clubs. The worst of all was Jumbo Courtney, a fellow subaltern, who was brought back from a sailing expedition with a lady in a very poor way indeed. It caused quite a sensation and news of it was included in the national press at home. The cause turned out to be the breakfast ham, the Danish tin being poisoned. When heads were counted in hospital it transpired that the Commanding Officer and Second-in-Command were there and all the junior officers, but no Captains. They had celebrated the departure of one of their number for home on the Saturday night and could not face breakfast on Sunday; so no ham and its disagreeable consequences for them.

A dinner party was held at a house where it transpired that a dog had contracted rabies. All those present, who included a non too popular senior officer of ours, had to undergo a very unpleasant course of injections, to our uncharitable amusement.

In addition, there was prickly heat, about which no one had warned me, but which caused considerable unexpected trauma.

Such were the perils of peacetime soldiering in India.

Food was mainly dull and disagreeable except for curry. I disliked it intensely at first but soon came to appreciate it in its hottest forms, which successfully disguised the lack of decent meat.

But many of the soldiers were never won over. It was a problem for the Orderly Officer attending meals at which curry was served and complaints made: 'Why don't you like it? It's very good.'

'What, eat "effing" wogs' food, Sir, not "effing likely!'

During all this time there had been an exchange of long, loving letters with my fiancée at home. The arrival of the Imperial Airways flying boats, which could be seen landing in Karachi harbour bringing the mail, was an eagerly awaited event. One day, not long before we were due to leave, came a letter saying that my fiancée was going to marry 'old Joe', some seventeen years her senior. She did not love him but he was wealthy and kind and would look after her in the way she wanted. She thought this was the best thing to do. In retrospect, seen from afar, perhaps she was right. But it did not feel like that at the time. I was absolutely shattered and wrote frantic letters in vain. I became sick at heart and was sent back to hospital. It was diagnosed as jaundice when I turned yellow.

The Battalion was now due to leave India, sailing on the last available troopship that year. It was deemed inadvisable to leave me behind alone so I was taken from the hospital and put on board. Christmas Day found me seasick on the Indian Ocean, suffering from jaundice, boils, and a broken heart and sharing a cabin with an uncongenial companion. I felt I had something in common with Job.

Jaundice entails a very strict diet but I got fed up with this and managed to persuade the Goanese cabin steward to bring me a proper meal, which I devoured eagerly. The result was disastrous, and I was delirious going up the Suez Canal. It was decided to off-load me at Port Said and send me to a hospital in the Canal Zone.

So I started 1938 by arriving in Port Said on a stretcher. The next time would be on the end of a parachute.

2

The Holy Land

An' I learned about women from 'er – Kipling.

Dawns in the Holy Land were to be plentiful, varied and exciting. The First Battalion of my Regiment had completed its overseas tour and sailed on home. The Second Battalion had been posted to Palestine. Those of us who had not completed our overseas tour were transferred from the First Battalion to the Second. After a lugubrious month in a military hospital at Ismailir on the Canal in Egypt, I was sufficiently recovered to make the journey across the Sinai Desert and join the Second Battalion at Haifa. The Battalion was stationed in a proper barracks just outside Haifa on a peninsula formed by the harbour on one side and the normal coastline on the other. The barracks were a great improvement on Karachi.

After the First World War, Great Britain was given a mandate by the League of Nations to administer Palestine, then the Holy or Promised Land. Indeed, promises about the ownership of this territory were the cause of the trouble. The Jews considered we had promised it to them, whilst the Arabs felt we had pledged it to them for their help in defeating the Turks in the First World War. Land was the bone of contention. The Jews had acquired by legal purchase much of the best and most fertile parts. These were sold to them by absentee landlords, 'fat cats' in Beirut and Damascus. The Palestinians, who had worked the land for many years, had mistakenly believed it was theirs and could not understand why they should be dispossessed. Although we were to be fighting them and many nasty incidents occurred which were perpetrated by gangs of Arabs, we had a certain sympathy for the locals whom we met in the villages when we patrolled the rugged countryside on which they struggled to make a living.

In January 1938 when the Second Battalion arrived, the Arab revolt was just beginning and grew in size and severity as the year progressed. Many of the activists were in gangs organised outside Palestine and inspired by the militant Mufti who was based in Damascus, a predecessor of the Khomenei of Iran. The Battalion was responsible for a large area of northern Palestine and was actively engaged in preventing acts of sabotage in and around Haifa, protecting many miles of railway line, also parts of the petroleum pipeline.

Not long after my arrival I was sent to take command of a detachment of about platoon strength at a village in the hills near the frontier called Mi'ilya. We lived in a large house and tents surrounded by stone walls, which we made ourselves plus sandbags and wire. The village was just a few hundred yards below. In the neighbourhood was a large old Crusader castle which was said to be used as a base by the rebels. Although quite near, it was a good two hours away on foot, up and down and across rugged country. We crept up there at night on a couple of occasions and surrounded it at dawn but we never found anyone there. The inhabitants of the village were predominantly Christian and the influence of the Crusaders was still in evidence as some of them had blue eyes, fair hair and freckles.

When I first got there it was still safe to motor along the hillside tracks and I used to visit the villages and call on the mukhtar, the head man, and try to make friends and perhaps get some information. As a rule, I was invited into his house to take coffee and knew that as long as I was enjoying his hospitality I was quite safe. One afternoon as I was sipping the strong black coffee in Tarshiha, an Arab rushed into the room and spoke in very agitated tones to my host. He became very alarmed and said I must leave at once. I rapidly drove out of the village and soon, in a narrow bit of the track, came upon some Arabs putting stones across it. They had not got very far and I charged them with the vehicle, bouncing over the rocks and getting away. There is very little doubt that had we been a few minutes, perhaps seconds, later we would have been ambushed and presumably written off. It was a very close thing.

This was proved to be so the following night when the camp was attacked, and fired on from positions in the rocks to the north of the post. The attack was successfully repulsed and none of us was hurt. When we examined the perimeter at dawn the next morning we found a blood-stained rag and some empty cartridge cases, proof that we had hit someone and that they had got quite close. The soldiers' morale was very high, but it was obvious that we had to be much more careful and we stood to in the good old military way at dawn. This was frequently distinctly unpleasant as we were quite high up and the weather was still cold, wet and miserable.

I told the village mukhtar that the open ground to the north of the camp was strictly out of bounds and that anyone seen there would be shot. Nevertheless, at dusk the next evening someone was seen there and, despite shouts of warning, refused to go, so he was shot. He was very badly wounded and could not be treated by us. I felt I could not leave him to die so organised an ambulance and a scout car and took him myself along the mountain tracks to the nearest medical facilities at Acre, about fifteen miles away. We had to come back along the same route in the dark and I must say I was very apprehensive, but fortunately we ran into a snow storm which was a blessing in disguise as it dispersed any attempt at an ambush. But it was really rather foolish.

It was apparent that there was definitely rebel activity in our area, and not far away a Royal Air Force Squadron Leader was ambushed and killed. One of my main preoccupations was to try and obtain more information about the rebels. The Christian inhabitants of our village were absolutely terrified and silent, but one day I was told that the child of one of my contacts had been badly burned or scalded when its mother upset a pot of boiling water over its legs. I took my Royal Army Medical Corps Orderly who came, quite voluntarily, to see the child. He was very good and managed to soothe him. Then for a few days we would visit them and he would treat the little boy with a solution, as I understood it, of very strong tea leaves on a bandage. Whatever it was it did the trick and he got better. The family were genuinely very grateful and were prepared to talk a little about the rebels. Possibly too much credence was given to their information but, added to other items that came in, it was apparent that a gang was active in our area. So Brigade decided to mount a full-scale operation based on us. No contacts were made as the rebels no doubt flitted quickly over the frontier, but at least the whole area was cleaned up and there were no more incidents for a while.

We then went back to Haifa and became part of a flying column which was organised to deal with any incidents and emergencies which might occur in northern Palestine. This sometimes took the form of escorting a tracker dog from the scene of an ambush into the rugged countryside with a long approach march, and then surrounding a village by night and entering it at dawn in the hope of catching the perpetrators of the ambush. The dog would lead us to a house but the villains had always fled. It was then decreed that we should blow up the house as an example to the inhabitants of the village. It never seemed to me to be of much use as all it did was to make a family homeless and add to the potential recruits for the roving gangs. However, that was what was done.

The business of escorting the tracker dog was a very arduous one for the troops concerned. While the valuable dog lolloped along the track at the bottom of the valley, the escorting soldiers had to make their way along the tops of the hills above, across very rugged and rocky terrain. In the parable of the sower, it was said that some seed fell on stony ground. We felt that it could hardly miss because it all seemed like stony ground to us. As the year developed, operations became more dangerous and sometimes a relatively small force found itself engaged by a large gang of well over a hundred. This basically suited us as we could engage the enemy instead of hitting and missing in thin air as so frequently happened. In our first sizeable action, thirty terrorists were killed and many wounded and several decorations earned. But it was not without casualties to ourselves.

When living in the barracks there were many lighter moments. Haifa itself had some very good restaurants and just down the coast from the barracks was the Casino. Cabaret acts of varying talent which travelled round the Middle East appeared there, and best of all there was a very good resident band with whom I made friends and joined the Cabaret very late at night or in the early morning. One snag was that the camp was frequently sealed from midnight until dawn and no one allowed in. So one either had to wait till dawn, or walk along the shore and get wet feet creeping round the wire at the edge of our barracks on the tip of the peninsula. This could easily be done and doesn't say very much for our security.

I met an old friend from Cambridge, Colin Maxwell, who was serving with the Palestine Police. After the war he became the police adviser to the Sultan of Muscat and Oman and practically ran the place. But in 1938 he gave one the entrée to Palestinian society which one would not otherwise have met, and I was fortunate enough to make the acquaintance of a very gorgeous Hungarian/Jewish lady. She was red-headed and if not 'mean', certainly 'moody and magnificent'. We rapidly became very close and once again dawn played its part. Curfews became frequent in Haifa and so it was not possible to leave a flat in the suburbs before dawn. In fact it was said that one part of the Standing Orders for the Guard Commander at Peninsula Barracks read 'At dawn open the gates for Lieutenant Crook returning from night ops'.

These glad interludes had to be sandwiched between many military activities. One of them started in rather an unusual way. One morning I was alone in the ante-room of the Officers' Mess when the waiter came in and announced a visitor. Naturally I welcomed him and offered him a drink, which he refused. He was stiff and awkward and difficult to talk to and I was relieved when the CO came in and took him over. I thought he must be a representative of one of the Church Societies, of whom we had a number passing through. I was therefore very surprised to meet this same person in the CO's office after lunch, and to learn that he was a certain Captain Orde Wingate who had a mandate from the GOC to

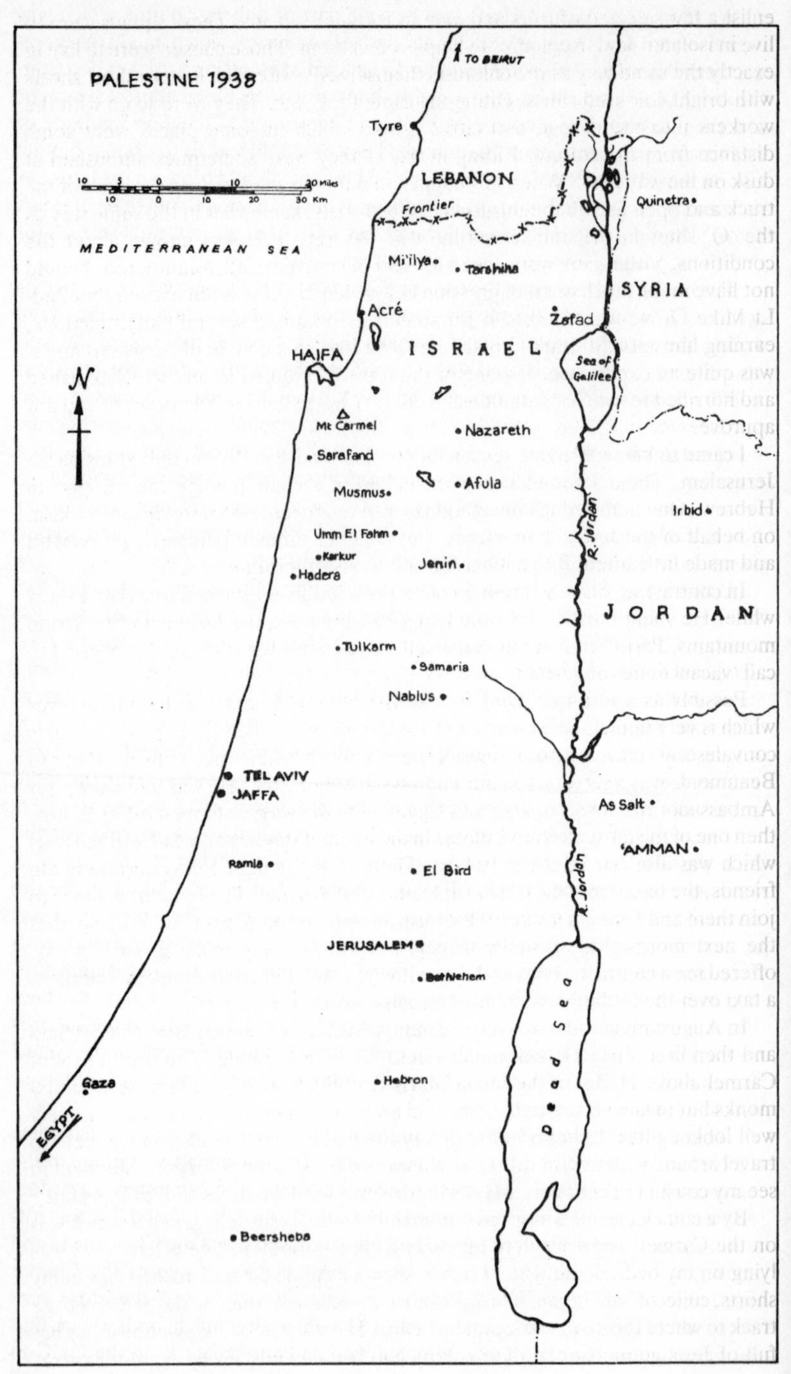
PALESTINE 1938
TO BEIRUT
Tyre
LEBANON
10 5 0 10 20 Miles
10 0 10 20 30 Km
Frontier
MEDITERRANEAN SEA
Mi'ilya
Tarshiha
SYRIA
Quinetra
Acré
Zefad
HAIFA
ISRAEL
Sea of Galilee
N
Mt Carmel
Nazareth
Sarafand
Afula
Musmus
Irbid
Umm El Fahm
Karkur
Jenin
Hadera
R. Jordan
JORDAN
Tulkarm
Samaria
Nablus
TEL AVIV
JAFFA
As Salt
'AMMAN
Ramla
El Bird
JERUSALEM
Bethlehem
Dead Sea
Hebron
Gaza
EGYPT
Beersheba

enlist a few selected officers and men to form 'Q' squads. These squads were to live in isolated Jewish colonies to help protect them. Those chosen were to live in exactly the same way as the colonists themselves, *ie* dressing in very short shorts with bright coloured shirts, eating the same food, etc. They were to go with the workers into the orange and citrus groves which in some places were some distance from the colony. Riding in trucks they were sometimes ambushed at dusk on the way back. When this happened our men were to drop the sides of the truck and open fire on the unsuspecting terrorists, somewhat in the same way as the 'Q' ships in the anti-submarine war. As yet, little was known about the conditions. Volunteers were asked for and of course we all volunteered. I could not have made much of an impression before lunch as I was not chosen, but 2nd-Lt Mike Grove was. He did it for some time and had several gallant actions, earning himself a Military Cross. I replaced him on a couple of occasions and it was quite an experience. On one of them the CO joined us and was astonished and horrified to see Wingate punch a dilatory horse hard on the nose: he did not approve.

I came to know Wingate reasonably well and once called on him at his flat in Jerusalem. There I found him stark naked in a chair reading the Talmud in Hebrew. One admired his unorthodox, inspired ideas and energetic enthusiasm on behalf of the Jewish community, but he was a difficult person to get on with and made little attempt to endear himself to his subordinates.

In contrast we had a charming young French officer attached to us for a short while. He spent most of his time living rough among the Druses in the Syrian mountains. Periodically he took himself off to Beirut for what he was pleased to call 'vacances de congestion'.

Possibly as a result of living in a Jewish colony, I contracted Dengue fever which is very unpleasant. I was sent to Sarafand hospital and then given a week's convalescent leave. I took myself off to Syria where my cousin, Richard Beaumont, was a secretary in our embassy at Damascus. (He was to become our Ambassador in Morocco, Iraq and Egypt.) On the way, I stopped off at Beirut, then one of the most attractive places in the world. I stayed at the St George Hotel which was also one of the very best. There to my delight I discovered my old friends, the band from the Casino at Haifa, were playing. They encouraged me to join them and I was on my very best form and proved quite a hit. So much so, that the next morning the hotel manager, not knowing my military connections, offered me a contract to stay and sing with the band. I hurriedly took myself off in a taxi over the Cedar Mountains of Lebanon to Damascus.

In August my mother arrived in Haifa, travelling by banana boat to Port Said and then in a ropey old aeroplane across the desert. I lodged her up in Mount Carmel above Haifa, in the Stella Maris Hostel which was a monastery run by monks but in fact very suitable. She had a very pleasant room and was extremely well looked after. In her inimitable way she made many friends and was able to travel around with Christian Arabs in a way we could not possibly do. She went to see my cousin in Damascus and saw both Syria and Jordan, as well as Palestine.

By a coincidence, I was given command of one of our detachments which was on the Carmel range not very far away from my mother. One afternoon I was lying on my bed resting when I heard shots in the distance. I rushed out in my shorts, collected any soldiers I could find with their weapons and dashed down the track to where the firing could still be heard. There a grim scene awaited us. A bus full of Jews going back to their colony had been ambushed by Arab terrorists.

There was a guard of three armed Jews, two of whom had been killed, but one was still firing. The gang was about to finish them all off when we arrived but we drove them away, killing seven and capturing two. We also recovered two rifles and a large quantity of ammunition. Fortunately we were able to save the occupants of the bus, though two women were wounded, one of whom was pregnant. It transpired that the gang had intended to take over the bus, drive it up to the unsuspecting colony and attack it. Our prompt and successful action was deemed to have averted a considerably greater tragedy.

Fortunately, my mother was away in Syria at the time and when she came back we were able to enjoy some very pleasant times with my friends in Haifa before she went back after six weeks in the country.

During September the extent of the Arab revolt reached serious proportions and there were not many troops to contain it. I was detailed to enlist and train a Jewish Company to support us. Accompanied by a Sergeant, I went to Tel Aviv to do this. There, after a short period of concentrated and vigorous training, I had the eerie experience of marching down the main street of Tel Aviv amidst large crowds who were lining the route and clapping.

We managed to contain the revolt, and after Munich the War Office was able to release more troops and a whole division was sent out. They all came through the port of Haifa and for a while I was busily employed in helping them and their stores disembark. This did allow me nights in Haifa, which were not wasted.

Then I was sent to take over a company detachment which protected a large Jewish colony, Kerkur, some miles to the south of Haifa. There I was visited by the Divisional Commander, a short, fierce little man. He asked me a lot of searching questions but seemed satisfied with my answers. Then he pointed to a feature behind us and said 'Where is that?' It was Mount Carmel and I thought to myself that even after only a short time in Palestine, if you don't know where that is, you don't know very much. I was not very impressed and at that time the name B.L. Montgomery meant nothing to me.

Dawn military activities interspersed with return journeys from my girlfriend's flat continued apace. Christmas found me staying with her in Jewish Jerusalem where we bought a beautiful puppy like a miniature panda, outside King David's Gate. Shortly after this I returned to Jerusalem to take a colloquial arabic test. The night before the exam I was in the King David Hotel when I received an urgent telephone call from the Adjutant saying that I must come back at once to catch a troopship. I had been appointed Adjutant of our Regimental Depot at Maidstone and this was the only ship which would get me back in time. So I never took the arabic exam, which was just as well as my friend Jumbo Courtney did not pass and he was much more proficient at it than I was.

There was a very tearful farewell with the lady and the puppy in Haifa and then I was off after a very full year, during which I had grown up and learned much about my profession, as well as the fair sex.

3

Preparing for War

Back to the Army again – Kipling.

A Regimental Depot before the war was a pleasant place to be. Its role was to enlist and train recruits for the regular units and it acted as both home and heart of the Regiment. The small permanent staff were carefully selected and it came as a very pleasant surprise to be nominated as Adjutant at a comparatively early age. Maybe I owed this to my faithless fiancée. Not long before, the previous holder of the post had an affair with the wife of a very distinguished member of the county establishment, which caused some dismay. Perhaps my monastic behaviour in India, whilst being faithful to my then love, may have had some bearing on the issue. Also I played cricket. Anyway there I was on the bottom rung of the staff ladder and, after starting with some trepidation, found I was good at it. The Commanding Officer was the crusty Major of Karachi days who disapproved of the singing, and we trod warily around each other for a while. But after a short period of mutual suspicion, we found that we complemented each other very well: I served him to the best of my ability and he accepted me. I became devoted to him.

A car was a necessity. I nearly bought an old Rolls Royce for £40 but ducked it; pity really. Two-seater sports cars were hardly commodious, so that soon went in favour of a sedate Hillman family saloon. A well organised officer travelled with a ground sheet and a rug and a vital piece of equipment then discreetly known as a French Letter but now openly acclaimed as a condom, perhaps named after a fine French rugby player. So the French connection remains.

The old barracks at Maidstone were opposite the prison down by the river and were designed for one hundred and fifty, and there was no room for much expansion. One of my very first tasks was to find somewhere suitable for a large training centre. This was done when the Clerk of Works, Mr Golding, and I walked down the road to Chatham and found what we considered was a suitable site at Sandling Park. Eventually a camp was built there which is still in use.

In the summer of 1939, as the prospect of war became more evident, the Government instituted a call-up and we had the first batch of conscripts known as Militia. The press were very interested, to the horror of my CO, who could not abide or cope with them. The *Daily Mirror* decided to send its feature writer of the time to visit us and see how the young men were being treated. The feature writer was a lady called Eileen Ascroft who was a predecessor of Marjorie Proops. She was a colleague of my late fiancée, and I knew her well. Thus I was able to deal with her on friendly terms and we got a very good write-up, to my CO's relief. Later we had a visit from Godfrey Winn, who I also knew, and that went equally well. From then on I could do little wrong.

The Depot fielded a very good cricket team and had a good fixture list. Our main match was against the Maidstone Police, in those days an independent force. The Chief Constable, Mr Vann, used to seek out and enlist fast bowlers from his native Lancashire and then deploy them against us on a terrible pitch. Opening the batting against them was a most hazardous business. After this, playing against the Buffs on the county ground at Canterbury during an air raid seemed a safe pastime.

In the field of music and vocals a number of opportunities presented themselves. First, one evening, as a party of young officers we took ourselves to the Palais de Dance at Rochester, a large dance hall with a decent band. Whilst we were there, a crooning competition from local amateur talent was announced. My companions chivvied me into entering and, to my surprise, I won on popular applause. I was pleased to be presented with a handsome prize, but not so pleased when the local reporter turned up and asked my name. It was obvious that I was military so, thinking quickly, I replied 'Lieutenant Smith, the Buffs'. This was just as well as it duly appeared in the local rag and my CO, if he had seen my name, would not have been amused.

Not long after war was declared I found myself in the Café Anglais in Leicester Square with David Rooke, who had just been presented with his MC at the Palace which he had won in Palestine. This time we were in uniform. We had a table near Harry Roy's band, in fact next to Ray Ellington, the drummer. I was humming their numbers with obvious pleasure when Ray passed me the microphone. I continued regardless and was then received with applause. Perhaps it was the uniform which led to the success. People put up with a lot in those days. I subsequently sang there several times with Harry Roy's 'Playmates', *ie* his wife Princess Pearl and her sister, and managed to hold my own.

The main scene for my vocalising in the war was Hatchetts in Piccadilly. This was normally a good, expensive, staid restaurant with no music. It also had a small bar which one visited to drink pink gins with old 'Kohais' from India and West Africa. One day I went into the bar and was thrilled and astonished to hear some magnificent swing music coming up from the restaurant below. On inspection I found it was pianist/composer Arthur Young and violinist Stephane Grappelli practising in the style of the Hot Club of France, with Chappy D'Amato on guitar. Stephane had just got out from Paris and become a regular feature of Hatchetts.

One evening we went to a party at Stephane's flat before going to Hatchetts. I knocked on the door, which was opened very cautiously by Stephane. 'Ah, Paul, that is OK. Come in. There is this terrible woman, you see, who won't leave me alone. Please help to protect me from her.' 'Of course,' I replied, 'but how?' 'When she comes I will hide in the cupboard and you will tell her I am not here.' 'OK.'

Sure enough a little later there came a loud banging on the door and a woman's voice crying, 'Let me in Stephane, I know you are there!'

After seeing that Stephane was safely hidden, I opened the door and told her that Stephane was not with us. 'I know he is,' she insisted and pushed past me. However, she could not see him, and I assured her that he had already gone to Hatchetts. Angry and suspicious she reluctantly left. 'Well done, Paul,' said Stephane emerging from his cupboard, 'you have saved my life. She's a terror, that one.'

Hatchetts also boasted a super swing band. After a bomb had hit the Café de Paris the survivors of Snake Hips Johnson's band formed its nucleus. All the best jazz players in London came along late in the evening, some of them being musicians with the Guards. In the time of the Blitz it was sometimes impossible to get home late at night and people stayed on, making and listening to music. This was where I came in, as hard worked musicians were glad to have someone – anyone – to help them fill in the long hours of the early morning. Whenever I could during the war, I performed there. I did not pay for my supper but sang for it. Mr Gerauld, the restaurant manager, encouraged this and was kindness itself in that he always had a table for me and never gave me a bill. Thus I was able to entertain a succession of young ladies in fine style.

So what was so special about my music? I tried to be a jazz singer which has been defined by Billie Holliday, one of its greatest exponents, as 'one who puts the voice into music like another instrument, and doesn't treat everything else as backing or accompaniment, and takes its song and moves it around so that it doesn't die but swings. You try to do something to a simple melody without spoiling it.'

Perhaps I managed to achieve this in some small way at a time when it was popular. Anyway, I got away with it and had a lot of enjoyment which may at times have been shared by others.

On the declaration of war life became very hectic indeed as we worked non-stop. The reservists poured in from everywhere and had to be processed and posted on to regular units. The Territorial Army units were expanded and needed reinforcements from our regular members of the Regiment. At the same time, the Depot expanded from 150 recruits to 1,500 who were being trained from scratch. The camp at Sandling was only just beginning to be built and so for over a year all the recruits had to be billeted out in the houses around the barrack area in Maidstone. So far as one can remember, there were no complaints which speaks volumes for the good behaviour of the young soldiers and the efficiency of the billeting staff, led by Reg Love. My own staff was superb, with Bill Stitt and Paddy Mullin as the mainstays and I acquired a pretty little secretary, an ATS girl called Mary Logan. Her mother was in command of the platoon of ATS, all volunteers, who did invaluable work and we would not have been able to cope without them. People on the Supplementary Reserve List turned up who had to be made into presentable officers very quickly. They included Philip Mackie, the well-known playwright; Dicky Dover, later parachutist and author; and Ken Scott, brother of Harold, a cricket and golf Blue.

One afternoon I was rung up direct by the infantry posting officer in the War Office, in itself an unusual occurrence. He said, 'I am sending you another Supplementary Reserve Officer, and this one is a bit different.' 'Not to worry,' I replied, 'we can cope with anybody by now, however different.' 'Well,' he continued, 'this one is indeed very different. I'm warning you now so you won't be shocked when he arrives.' 'So what's the problem?' I asked. 'I have to tell you that he is black, but his qualifications and background are excellent: he is a very nice fellow and I know you will treat him properly, which is why I am sending him to you.' 'OK,' I said, 'we'll look after him.'

I genuinely have never had any colour prejudice, but in 1939 it was unique to take a black officer into an English County Regiment. So the next day 2nd-Lieutenant Joe Moody presented himself to his Adjutant, and I like to think I was particularly welcoming and helped him settle into the Regiment. He was indeed both very black and a very nice fellow who proved himself a very competent officer, survived the war, and I was to meet him again many years later in Jamaica, where he graciously welcomed me in return.

It was a great time for marriages. First, Kip Keenlyside married his Jean, home from Karachi. Kip was a magnificent training subaltern and a very dear friend. If life was gloomy, Kip would only have to walk into the ante-room and it cheered up. It was a great loss when he went off to the TA. Next was Dennis Talbot who married Barbara. Dennis was to escape from France in a rowing boat and eventually became a Major-General and Colonel of the Regiment. Others at the time included Ken Scott and Tony Douglas, my assistant adjutant; also Robert Moss, my predecessor. For myself, I was immune. To tell the truth, I was probably still inwardly carrying a torch for my erstwhile fiancée. This anaesthetised me for several years and enabled me to 'love 'em and leave 'em' (apologies to those concerned).

But as the 'phoney war' progressed I became more and more restless and agitated that I, as a young officer, was stuck in England in a static unit, and tried everything to get to a fighting unit. I volunteered for anything that was going, including the newly forming parachutists but my CO said he could not spare me which was flattering but frustrating. Eventually there came an Army Council Instruction saying that officers were wanted for service in Africa and applications could not be withheld so I put forward mine, mentioning my phoney knowledge of Arabic. But the evacuation of the BEF from Dunkirk took place and Maidstone became, if not the front line, certainly the second. A force from the Infantry Training Centre, mainly recruits, together with the newly formed Home Guard, was organised under my Commanding Officer to check the German invaders if they succeeded in getting out of a bridgehead at the beaches. I remember well choosing sites on the approaches to Maidstone at which we would overturn trolley buses as a basis of road blocks. Meanwhile the surrounding airfields at Detling and West Malling were successfully attacked by the German airforce before Goebbels switched them to bombing London, and the Battle of Britain was fought out over our heads. Exciting days, and there was no thought of going anywhere else nearer the war.

To my chagrin and dismay the War Office churned out its paper and a Posting Order came appointing me as a Staff Captain in Africa. But not the African Desert of Egypt and Libya as I had intended, but West Africa.

So in Autumn 1940 I sailed off into the sunset leaving England at the height of the Blitz of which I had experienced only a part.

4
Wartime

We'll make you soldiers yet – Kipling.

My vain attempts to get into the action had resulted in my leaving it behind in the United Kingdom, where my mother ran an ambulance station in Fulham and my father served in a Home Guard unit based at Battersea Park. It all goes to show the validity of the basic military maxim 'never volunteer'. I only did once more. British West Africa in 1940 was a non-operational theatre and wartime dangers were incurred only at sea, in getting there and back, which did involve some unwanted dawns. On the voyage out, a small draft of officers and men was embarked on an elderly Belgian passenger ship, normally employed in taking Belgians to the Congo. I was appointed ship's Adjutant and so allotted a cabin to myself which boasted a large four-poster double bed, sadly wasted. We sailed from Avonmouth and in the Bristol Channel were stopped by a fast Naval motor boat with a top secret envelope for our OC Troops. The contents stated that the allegiance of the Belgian Captain was uncertain and he might possibly try to join the Vichy French, so be on our guard, or words to that effect.

Well, what could a bunch of poor Pongos at sea do about that? The OC Troops, Lieutenant-Colonel Tony Turner of the Suffolks, decided that the best we could do was to have a small picket always ready for instant duty to take over the ship! And an officer on the bridge, but we were to be discreet and ensure no offence was given. There were not many officers so we all took our turn on watch, thereby sharing the damp, stormy dawns. We were in convoy for a while but ships were reported being sunk off the coast of Ireland around us and the Captain increased our suspicions by insisting on leaving the convoy, saying that he could do better on his own. Soon we ploughed into a whole gale in the Atlantic, possibly a blessing in disguise, but it was misery for bad sailors. After this came days of cold, grey dawns with empty seas stretching all around and no sign of tropical conditions. We wondered whether one morning we would wake up in French controlled Dakar in Vichy West Africa, but after nearly three weeks we suddenly found ourselves arriving correctly off Freetown, Sierra Leone. There I expected to get off to become Staff Captain at Brigadier Michael Green's headquarters, who was a friend of my father. To my dismay I found my posting had been changed and I was to go on to Accra in the Gold Coast as a third grade staff officer at Headquarters Military Forces, West Africa.

I lived in a mud hut in the grounds of Achimota, the West African University, just inland from Accra. The role of Force Headquarters was to organise Colonial troops, first to defend the colonies against a highly unlikely, but not impossible, attack by our Vichy French neighbours and mainly to build up a force which could be satisfactorily employed in other theatres of war. Eventually two West African Divisions fought in Burma.

But the birth and growing pains were slow and tedious, involving detailed and finicky staff work and protracted negotations with both Whitehall and Colonial Governments. Not very exciting, as seen through the eyes of a lowly staff officer at Headquarters. There were not any operational dawns but we started the day with physical training at 6.45am, which was near enough to dawn to be uncomfortable. We worked from 7.15am frequently to 7.15pm in sweaty, tropical conditions, six days a week and sometimes seven. I managed to escape from the office sometimes to play football – soccer, not my normal game – with the soldiers. I achieved this by organising a military team to go round and play the local soccer sides in aid of the Spitfire Fund. This was great fun and we met some charming people full of enthusiasm and vigour. I once inadvertently kicked the bare foot of a nimble young African forward very hard indeed. I hobbled away having virtually broken my booted toe whilst he darted on regardless to score a goal. They also contributed generously towards a Fund for the purchase of a Spitfire aeroplane. We also had some very good cricket and hockey against teams from Achimota College.

As usual, music – my kind of music – produced another entertaining distraction. My very good friend, Jumbo Courtney of the Regiment, arrived from Maidstone to join the Gold Coast Regiment. Like me he was a great jazz follower. He could play the drums adequately and was no mean performer on the penny whistle from which he could produce 'hot licks' in the style of Benny Goodman. We discovered a really superb swing pianist called Jim Hutton who was quite brilliant. Together we formed a trio, with me as announcer, compere and singer, and performed at hops, and even on the local radio who were grateful for any reasonable material. I well remember announcing: 'This is ZOY calling with fifteen minutes of sweet swing – In a jam by the Army.' Other than this, Jumbo and I were not happy with soldiering in West Africa and both worked hard to escape. He was to help his brother, Roger Courtney, to create the early Special Boat Section and was to take part in many exciting clandestine operations, including taking United States Army Generals Mark Clark and Lemnitzer ashore in rubber boats from a submarine off North Africa, not far from Algiers, before the invasion. His adventures have been recorded elsewhere but Jumbo distinguished himself on this occasion by sneezing when they were hiding in a cellar, and then capsizing a canoe which contained 2,000 US dollars in gold. Jumbo and I were always meeting in the strangest places and we shall hear of him again.

One was worried by the news from the United Kingdom, or rather the lack of it, as communications were very variable and letters sometimes never arrived, having been sunk. My father's office was hit by a bomb, fortunately at night when no one was there. Meanwhile, I beavered away as a reluctant staff officer in the sun. The only dangers, apart from tropical diseases, were being driven at high speed by our charming GOC-in-C, General Sir George Giffard, round Nigeria when I accompanied him on a tour there. I was impatient of the tempo and (to me) the absurd nit-picking of detailed staff work and at times clashed with my superiors. However, they bore with me, taught me my staff duties, promoted me and sent me back to the Staff College in England.

So after fifteen months 'on the Coast' I returned to the perils of the sea in January 1941. In order to catch a convoy from Freetown, Sierra Leone, I emplaned on one of the few transport aircraft in Africa which was out there at the time. Its short range was limited to the necessity to land and refuel at Monrovia in

Liberia, the only neutral state around. At Freetown, I was fortunate enough to embark on the flagship of the Elder Dempster Line, a very comfortable passenger ship. She was also the headquarters ship of a large, slow convoy with the convoy commander, a retired Royal Navy Commodore, and his signal staff on board. Passengers were mainly civilians escaping from Africa and we few military men took our turn in manning an anti-aircraft machine-gun post located just above the bridge. From there one could see the convoy commander and his signaller in action, supported by three frigates shepherding the elderly cargo boats like sheepdogs with their flock. It was an interesting experience to go up there at dawn and count the ships to see if they were all still with us; there should have been thirty-nine in all. The Bay of Biscay was pleasantly calm and uneventful, but as we reached the Western Approaches a German spotter plane was seen in the vicinity and we feared the worst. However, at this time the German cruisers *Scharnhorst* and *Gneisnau* decided to break out from Brest and make their dash down the Channel. Thus all German resources were concentrated on protecting them and we got home slowly and peacefully without incident. It shows that it is indeed an ill wind that blows no one any good.

At the Staff College I was again in luck as I was posted to the Division stationed at Minley Manor, an imitation French château in lovely gardens and grounds, some three miles south of Camberley. The quartermaster there was Lieutenant-Colonel Jack Coe of the Regiment and, assisted by him and the Divisional Commander's secretary, with whom I established an affectionate liaison, I managed to acquit myself well and land a plumb job, *ie* Brigade Major.

The War Office posting machine was, as usual, in good form and I was sent as the only student from West Africa (the other one didn't survive the course) to a brigade just returned from Iceland. I knew all about mules and malaria and they were expert in snow ploughs and frostbite. Once again I was to live in a tent, never a good idea and certainly not in mid-Wales in a wet September. The Division, 49 West Riding, was mainly composed of sturdy territorial soldiers from Yorkshire and as yet was very little changed after spending eighteen months together in Iceland. My Brigade, 147 Infantry Brigade, was made up of a battalion of the West Yorkshire Regiment and two battalions of the Duke of Wellington's Regiment. But by great good luck our affiliated artillery regiment turned out to be 143 Field Regiment (Kent Yeomanry) based on Maidstone, whose mobilisation I had helped with when at the Depot. So I had friends in the artillery which is a great asset for an infantry brigade major.

In those days the brigade staff was small with only one major – a brigade major – who was virtually chief of staff of the brigade group. The Brigadier was a charming Irish Guardsman, Edmund Mahoney, who was an excellent infantry soldier and a very efficient trainer of infantry but had little knowledge of, or interest in, the capabilities of other units which came to make up a brigade group such as anti-tank artillery, engineers and all the supporting administrative units. During the many exercises in which we took part he left their employment mainly to me. The Staff Captain was John Driver of the Duke of Wellington's Regiment, who became my very dear friend and later my solicitor. Another friend was the Signal Officer, Gus Wolff, who came from a family firm of tin brokers.

The wretched Brigade Major endeavoured to communicate with Division and the Units in the Group by dashing from one wireless set to another. These were not then located in one comfortable command vehicle but in the backs of vehicles parked in different places scattered around a muddy farmyard or field. This could be pretty arduous in the blackout on a dark, wet night and led to many exhausting dawns.

Training in the United Kingdom during 1943 was very intensive. The West Riding Division was originally commanded by Major-General Curtis who, along with a number of very worthy territorial officers, was deemed to be a bit too elderly and nice to cope with the pace of active warfare. He was replaced by Major-General 'Bubbles' Barker, a very vigorous and efficient general who rapidly smartened us up considerably. A fire-eater, he was in some respects not unlike General Montgomery and so we were able to cope when Monty took over command of 21 Army Group and came to inspect us.

For an awful period the Division was trained in a snow-and-mountain warfare role amidst the Highlands of Scotland but happily was changed to a follow-up division for the invasion. Like the Duke of York's soldiers, we had some unexpected and unexplained moves. The whole brigade went from South Wales to Scotland, but returned again almost on arrival. Then we went back again to Scotland. The move of a brigade group which is about the size of a large village as part of a division, which in itself is the size of a small town, is quite a business but we got very expert at it. From Scotland we went to an area around Yarmouth before finally moving to our assembly areas for the Invasion.

5

Invasion

The backbone of the Army is the non-commisioned man – Kipling.

It was a strange feeling to wake up at dawn on 6 June 1944 and fine oneself still in a vehicle park near Barking, London, whilst one's comrades were battling it out on the beaches in Normandy, the beaches which one had studied so carefully and often. It was frustrating and worrying but there was nothing to be done as we were a follow-up division now and our transport ship could not get away from London docks until tomorrow at the earliest.

It was strange, too, to see vehicles parked closely all around us, a magnificent target for air attack but we were never to see enemy aircraft in the sky above us, such was our mastery of the air.

At this time 147 Infantry Brigade consisted of two battalions of the Duke of Wellington's Regiment and one battalion of the Royal Scots Fusiliers which had replaced the West Yorks during the past year. When Monty arrived to take over 21 Army Group he soon decreed that any commanding officer over the age of forty should be replaced and we lost two COs in the Dukes. No doubt he was right, yet we were to lose the services of an extremely stalwart person who had the affection and confidence of all his soldiers and was tough as blazes. It transpired that without him his battalion was not as effective as it might have been.

There was nothing to do in this assembly area except wait and it dawned on me that nearby Barking station was at this end of the District Line and Wimbledon, the home of my parents, at the other. Security was no longer a factor as the landing places in Normandy were now common knowledge and no longer a closely guarded secret. So I decided to fill in the time by getting on the tube and visiting my parents at Wimbledon, whom I had not seen for some time. So I did just that and to my parents' delighted astonishment turned up at their home, Little Manor, near Wimbledon Lawn Tennis Club, to celebrate my mother's birthday on a date which would no longer ever be forgotten. It was all good stiff-upper-lip stuff and my parents soon calmly sent their only son back on his way to war. I remember my mother saying: 'Just do your duty wherever and whatever it may be.'

The good old District Line duly returned me to the transit camp in Barking and the next day we made the short journey in our now waterproofed vehicles to the nearby London docks and embarked on one of the Fort class newly built transport ships. I was OC Troops and the First Officer very kindly offered me his bunk in his cabin.

Later we sailed down the Thames at night and before dawn I was awakened by a loud crash, and the noise of the engines had stopped. Hastening to the bridge I learned that something had hit the ship, gone through the bridge and damaged the steering. We dared not move as we were then in the Straits of Dover in the mineswept channel and this was strictly limited with mines close on both sides.

This dawn found us hove to in dangerous waters within sight and range of German guns in France. Two German fighters did dive to strafe us but happily went along on either side ~~of the ship~~ and caused no damage or casualties, but it seemed that after two years of intensive training for war I was destined not even to reach it. However, after some anxious hours the steering was repaired. Meanwhile, a sailor down below in the engine room struck something which should not have been there and it was found to be an unexploded missile. It turned out to be one of the early German flying bombs which happily had failed to explode so far. We had some tame Sappers on board and they were invited to dispose of it. It was not their role but they bravely and skilfully hauled it out and dropped it over the side of the ship to the cheers of all on board.

So we were now able to proceed slowly on our way to the beachhead where we arrived some twelve hours late. There was very little activity and we could not persuade any landing craft to take any interest in us but eventually a passing American landing craft agreed to take some of our vehicles ashore. After a short trip we came to a halt and the Captain said: 'Gee Major, reckon this is as far as we can go.' The front of the landing craft was lowered and it appeared that the shore was as far away as ever. We had come to a halt on a sand bank. My vehicle went out first into a few inches of water but after a very short while plunged down into over four feet of water, coming over the driver's and my seats, but we ploughed on and reached the sand safely, as did all the other vehicles. There was not a soul in sight and it was a quiet evening at dusk. It had been impressed on us during briefing that under no circumstances should we de-waterproof the vehicles on the beach but to do so inland. However, after our adventurous journey they were all spluttering and coughing and the engines were very overheated, so I took the initiative and decided to de-waterproof there and then. After doing this we went inland. An early example that little happens in war as anticipated or planned.

I came to the conclusion that we had arrived on Gold Beach on the extreme left flank of the beachhead when we should have been considerably further to the West on Sword. I took my convoy off and, navigating along tracks remembered from a lengthy study of air photos before the invasion, arrived intact in the assembly area which had been allotted to us and met up with the troops and the Brigadier, much to his relief. This was done in the dark without lights and I was rather pleased with my navigation.

We hung around in the bridgehead for a bit and were subjected to a little bombing at night which I hated, though it was nothing compared with what my parents and the citizens of Britain had endured during the Blitz. I did not mind too much being shot at or shelled but hated bombing. The Intelligence Officer at Brigade HQ was an important member of the team, especially to the Brigade Major. I had selected a person who filled the bill admirably. First he was very neat and painstaking and marked a map beautifully. Next he played 'a boogy-woogy piano' superbly; finally he was ostensibly more frightened than I was which was good for morale, mine if not his.

We were sent to take over part of the line near the village of Cristot. Attack was the order of the day. Our first attack by the Scots Fusiliers was successful but the next one, by 6th Dukes, less so and they suffered severe casualties, particularly among officers. This battalion was singularly unfortunate and suffered casualties wherever it went, even during a pay parade which was hit by shelling when they were in reserve. In two weeks they lost twenty-three officers including the CO, Ken Exham, and all the company commanders and 350 other ranks. They were subjected to a particularly vicious and efficient counter-attack by 12 Panzer SS Division which resulted in an unplanned withdrawal. By the end of June morale was at rock bottom and early in July they were withdrawn and replaced by 1 Leicesters. This battalion was commanded by Lieutenant-Colonel Tony Novis, an English rugby international and an old Uppinghamian. In fact, many of the officers were from Uppingham and known to me.

June was spent in tough but ineffectual fighting in Bocage country against determined and brilliantly handled German troops. At one time we were up against the crack 12 SS PZ Division and later we fought against a 'stomach' battalion whose fighting qualities were derided by the intelligence staffs at higher headquarters. All I can say is that they should have come and fought against them themselves. These unfortunate Germans with stomach troubles were well sighted in positions from whence they could not leave as they would have been shot by their tough regular NCOs behind them. Thus they remained firing at us from their dugouts until we literally trod on them, causing unnecessary casualties, particularly amongst leaders.

We had very good support from the tanks and their crews of the Sherwood Rangers Yeomanry who did their best but were no match for the German Tiger tanks, and infantry tank co-operation was not as good as it should have been in this difficult country.

A major attack in conjunction with other formations of XXX Corps was launched at the end of June and we succeeded in capturing our main objective, the village of Rauray but at a cost, as I have previously indicated.

Early in July, in addition to the replacement of 6DWR by 1 Leicesters, we also changed commanders. Our Irish Brigadier, although physically brave as a lion, could not mentally cope with the complexities of handling a brigade group and armour in action, and started to do some very strange things. Fearing for the safety of the soldiers, I had to report these to the GSO 1 at Division, Dick Jelf. The Brigadier did in fact suffer a nervous breakdown and was abruptly invalided home. On a quiet afternoon I was dozing in the command vehicle when an old friend from West Africa days appeared at the back, Henry Wood. I knew he was commanding a battalion of the Queens somewhere else in the bridgehead but did not expect to see him in our area. 'What are you doing here?' I asked. 'I'm sorry Paul but I've come to be your Brigadier,' he replied. 'Welcome, sir, how splendid.' It was indeed, as Henry Wood was a very high grade officer in all respects, as well as a friend.

Also on 3 July, Lieutenant-Colonel Montgomery-Cunningham, the massive, unflappable, splendid CO of 11 RSF, was killed. His Jocks adored him and he was a tremendous loss. He was replaced by Duncan Eykyn, a friend of mine from Staff College days. Three battalion commanders had been written off in less than a month, and the only CO to survive was Felix Wolsey with the 7th Dukes. He was an outstanding commanding officer, always courteous and kindly as well as brave and very efficient. He was always thinking of his men and others and was one of the very best COs, and happily did survive throughout.

There were other changes at Headquarters also. John Driver, our splendid Staff Captain, left to go to the Staff College. But we were reinforced by a new General Staff Officer, a welcome addition to the establishment. To our delight the officer concerned was Jack Crosland from the Staff College where we had sent him six months previously. He was a great character, a lively officer and very good value; and on 10 July we acquired a piano for the Intelligence Officer, which thereafter was given pride of place in a captured truck and never left us.

So we battled on, with emphasis on active patrolling. This was controlled by Brigade and we did our best to make sure by careful planning that there were no unfortunate mistakes and misunderstandings causing unnecessary casualties. I made it a practice to take the night's patrol programme personally to the battalions concerned. It gave me a chance to get away from the Headquarters, find out how the troops were faring, and have a chat with the commanding officers, who were glad of an opportunity to unburden themselves.

Most activity began just before or at dawn regularly when the results of the night's patrols came in and we were prepared for a possible enemy counter-offensive. Some nights were quiet and it was possible to get some sleep but often this was not so. Sleep became a big problem for key personnel, particularly commanders, and it became necessary that they should be instructed to take periods of rest and stick to them.

After a massive effort by other formations, Caen and its outskirts were captured and some regrouping took place. 49 Division became part of 1 British Corps which in itself was included in the Canadian First Army. In mid-July we were moved to an area south-east of Caen expecting to act as a follow-up infantry division behind a breakthrough by the armour. But in the event it was some three weeks before this could take place.

6
Breakout

We rolled upon them like a flood and washed their ranks away – Kipling.

The scene which awaited us at dawn outside Caen after a tricky night move around the city was very different from that which we had become accustomed to in the fields and hedgerows of the Bocage country. Behind were the ruins of the shattered city of Caen though happily the towers of the Abbeys were mostly intact. Nearer were the skeletons of large factories in the outskirts of Colombelles. The terrain consisted mainly of open cornfields which had been cut and we set about digging in our positions in the stubble. It was not until nightfall that the real difference became evident. Apart from increased shelling and bombing we were divebombed throughout the night, not by German aircraft but by French mosquitoes. Trying to sleep in a slit trench was literally a nightmare, perpetually disturbed by the buzzing of the wretched insects and the subsequent itching of bites. The only solution was to cover up every part of one's skin and sweat it out. No one had expected an attack of this scale by mosquitoes in Northern Europe and there were none of the anti-mosquito sprays and ointments available as there would be in the Far East. We were literally covered with bites and a few men were so badly bitten around the eyes that they had to be evacuated as medical casualties.

We were on the extreme eastern corner of the Allied Line based at Cagny and as such received much enemy attention. We were told that we were the nearest troops to Paris, but it was to be General Bradley's American troops who were to be the first there as a result of their successful breakout on the right flank. So while we fought on against a determined and skilfully handled enemy without dramatic progress or publicity, Patton's troops enjoyed a startling and very lightly opposed advance with the consequent excited press attention. Although naturally envious, I don't think we minded very much so long as someone was defeating the Germans and bringing the fighting nearer to an end. Subject as we were to shelling from three sides, life was uncomfortable in addition to the mosquitoes and casualties inevitable. At the end of July Lieutenant-Colonel Tony Novis was wounded and replaced by Lieutenant-Colonel Donald Liddell, a GSO 2 from 49 Division HQ.

On 7 August an offensive was launched by the Canadian Army of which we were a part. It was preceded by a massive night air-attack by Bomber Command which succeeded in destroying all the villages and consequently blocking the roads. A further air bombardment took place the next day in daylight and was a disaster, as we witnessed the Polish Armoured Division being decimated alongside us. This 'short bombing' was to be repeated a week later owing to a mix-up about the colour of smoke used for identification of our own troops which seems unforgivable. Fortunately for us we were not involved in these tragic mistakes. We managed to capture our objective, Vimont, and did not play a very active part in the assaults which were to cost the participating units dear. The morale of the Canadians became low, but under our splendid GOC, 'Bubbles' Barker, we were not aware of this. Eventually the dam broke and the hinge, of which we formed part, creaked open. We visited the edge of the Falaise Gap and saw for ourselves the heartening but gruesome evidence of an army in defeat, bodies of men and horses everywhere, equipment, vehicles, guns abandoned, buildings destroyed and hedgerows scarred. Although the famous Falaise Gap was not in fact properly closed, the part which we saw indeed looked like a victory.

Then on 14 August Jack Crosland was killed by a shell at an OP less than a month after rejoining us from the Staff College. He was a great Yorkshire character and I still have his admirably kept Staff Officer's notebook. A week later a despatch rider, Lance-Corporal Sillitoe of the Brigade Signal Squadron, was killed. He had been with us for nearly two years and was a magnificent chap who would undertake to ride his motorcycle under any conditions in order to ensure an important message got through when other means failed. I had sent him on this mission and felt his loss, along with that of Jack, very badly.

And so we were on the move at last and pursued the enemy to the Seine. We advanced via Pont l'Eveque to Pont Audemer, crossing three rivers on the way. In fact we carried out three night river-crossings in five days. Although enemy resistance was very slight we could never take this for granted. Thus at each river, patrols had to be sent out to locate the enemy and then a full-scale night attack with its supporting fire plan arranged, assault boats allocated, the crossing made, and then the bridging equipment brought up. All this required a great deal of active staff work at Brigade Headquarters all through the night and one hardly slept for a week. Dawn was spent anxiously awaiting reports from the troops across the river. Happily, casualties were light, the further effects of mosquito bites and dysentry being the main items.

It was wonderful to be going forward and the countryside became rural and free from the ravages of war. In addition to crossing three rivers and one stream, we liberated many places in Normandy. I well remember the Château at Camberemer as a very pleasant place at which to come to rest, if only for a short while. We had by now established a good drill for setting up our HQ in the field and learned how to make ourselves comfortable. We added a consenting cow to the piano to accompany us. We were lucky enough to liberate a Benedictine monastery and the delighted monks were gracious enough to give us a liberal stock of their lovely liqueur.

At the end of August the leading infantry had crossed the Seine and Brigade HQ followed them later in 'Dukws', *ie* swimming trucks, which was a fascinating way to cross this big river at its mouth. We came to rest at a Château at Saineville, some ten kilometres to the east of Le Havre which we set about planning to capture.

7

Le Havre

You may hide in the caves, they'll be only your graves,
but you can't get away from the gun – Kipling.

Whilst we were crossing the Seine at the beginning of September, the High Command were contemplating crossing the Rhine into Germany and ending the war before Christmas. Meanwhile it became essential to open up Channel ports, as the Mulberries at the invasion beaches were now some 400 miles away from the leading troops. So the task of capturing Le Havre was given to the 1st Canadian Army, in effect to 1 British Corps consisting of 49 Division and 51 Highland Division on our right, happily returned from recapturing St Valery-en-Caux.

The port of Le Havre was a formidable place to attack, being one of the strongest fortresses of the Atlantic Wall. Three sides were protected by water, the Seine Estuary, the sea, and a flooded area. The approach from the east was made difficult by a flooded valley dominated by high ground, whilst a minefield and anti-tank ditch barred the approach from the north. There were many concrete strong points manned by infantry guarding the anti-tank ditch as well as gun positions in concrete casements. In the town itself were two forts and many road blocks, pillboxes and fortified houses, together with anti-aircraft and anti-tank guns. The strength of the garrison was estimated to be at least 8,000 including 4,000 artillery and anti-aircraft personnel and some 1,300 Naval personnel of doubtful fighting value.

It was clear to both sides that the attack had to be made from the north. To carry out the assault we were greatly strengthened by detachments of Flails (mine destroying tanks), Crocodiles (tank flame-throwers), Kangaroos (armoured personnel carriers), and assault engineers. It was the biggest collection of 'armoured funnies' ever assembled in one place.

The defences were softened up for two days before the assault by shelling from Royal Navy ships at sea and bombing by the Royal Air Force. From the Field of the Cloth of Gold we were able to watch with awe and pleasure two massive raids by the air forces on the defences. They were accurately carried out and had a heartening effect on the morale of our troops and consequent disheartening effect on the enemy. Captured prisoners subsequently stated that the bombing was very frightening but there were comparatively few casualties, both to the German troops and civilians, owing to the excellence of the dug-out shelters which had been constructed. The most important result was the breakdown of communications which prevented commanders from knowing what was going on and switching their resources and firepower.

Because of the need to breach the minefields the attack had to be carried out at night. And what a night! There were flail tanks flailing away, detonating some mines and missing others; armoured assault engineer vehicles were chuntering around and tanks following up; there were the noise and effects of our own supporting fire from a variety of weapons; finally, of course, there was the enemy who reacted strongly with everything he had got. Everywhere there was the din of battle, organised chaos and danger. Traffic control on the few routes not blocked by bombing and clear of mines was vitally important and was well carried out by Provost assisted by an anti-tank battery. Vehicles taken forward by the infantry were strictly limited.

The first attack was made at last light by 56 Infantry Brigade. We had to pass through them and capture a feature on the southern flank overlooking Harfleur. We started at 2300hrs with an attack by 1 Leicesters. The tracks were still found to be heavily mined and progress was slow. There were some anxious moments but by noon the battalion finally captured its objective east of the Foret de Montgeon and a vital bridge leading into the port. This delayed the attack by 11RSF but by determined patrolling and aggression they succeeded in capturing their first objective on the southern flank by early afternoon. They were then given the task of clearing the whole of the southern flank, which proved harder than expected owing to the number of strongpoints and fortified houses which had to be tackled.

7DWR advanced through Montivilliers in Kangaroos and dismounted at the bridge captured by the Leicesters; then, supported by a squadron of tanks, they set off into the city where they met with less resistance. The night in contrast to the previous one was generally quiet except for parties of the enemy trying to give themselves up.

The next morning the advance continued, 7DWR having the best of it when they succeeded in capturing underground shelters well stocked with looted stores and wine. The German defenders had believed in doing themselves well. But 11RSF on the southern flank continued to have a sticky time, encountering stiff opposition. It was not until late afternoon that they cleared the whole area at considerable cost in killed and wounded. At Brigade Headquarters, too, we suffered a sad loss when one of our best liaison officers, Lieutenant Ken Hounsfield, was killed by a mine when visiting a battalion. but by late afternoon the German Garrison Commander had had enough and surrendered, much to our joy. Thus in forty-eight hours the fortress of Le Havre had been reduced and over 11,000 prisoners were captured. Our casualties were some 500.

I hope I have not made it sound too easy, it certainly was not. Although he received plenty of support, in the end it was the British infantry soldier who had to go forward and attack fortified positions in the face of enemy fire. It was due to his dogged courage, determination and skill that such a successful outcome was so rapidly achieved.

For the next forty-eight hours there was a mood of euphoria everywhere, which is hard to believe now in view of what was to take place at Arnhem a few days later, but was quite positive then at Le Havre. In fact the very next day I was summoned to see the Divisional Commander, General 'Bubbles' Barker, who greeted me with: 'Paul, you have been a brigade major for nearly two years now and have done very well, but it's time you did something else.' My heart leapt and I hoped perhaps he was going to give me command of a battalion, but my hopes were dashed when he continued: 'I am afraid I can't give you a battalion as there aren't any vacancies and unlikely to be any now. All our transport has been sent forward and we are virtually grounded. As far as I can see the war is over for us.' How wrong he was proved to be when the Division went to the Island and spent the early months of 1944 in bitter fighting along the southern banks of the Rhine.

This he did not know then and continued: 'But the war against the Japs in the Far East will go on and that will be the place for people like you and me. I have just been offered a vacancy to send a good chap to represent us at the American Army Staff College in the States. It is a unique opportunity well worth taking and in the right direction.' I was rather taken aback but there was nothing much I could say except murmur pleased acceptance. I was told that there was not much time and that I would be given a seat on a plane to fly back to UK the next day. So it was goodbye to the Headquarters of 147 Brigade and all the people there I had come to know well and respect after training and fighting so closely together.

During our combined operations training at Inverary in Scotland I had become enamoured of a pretty little Wren in the Communications branch there, so on my return I immediately phoned her saying I had less than a week's leave, come at once. She replied: 'The only way I can get any leave is to get married.' 'OK,' I said, 'let's do that.'

So we were married on 18 September in Wimbledon church by the accommodating vicar, with the verger and an air raid warden as witnesses. Two days' honeymoon in the Ritz and I was off. A wartime marriage indeed.

For additional details concerning the capture of LE HAVRE see Appendix A.

8
God's Own Country

Steam down the river down to New Orleans – Jazz Classic

There were three of us from Commonwealth Armies sent to represent them at the United States Army Command and General Staff School at Fort Leavenworth, Kansas. One was a South African. This was the first time I had come in contact with a genuine South African and came to discover with surprise and dismay just how different in outlook and unattractive they could be.

Uncle Sam in the shape of the US Army decided we should see as much as possible of this big country and we travelled the length of it and half the breadth. So it came to pass that one evening I found myself 'way down the river in New Orleans' singing a little number called *Basin Street Blues* in Basin Street wearing His Majesty's uniform. How this came about will be disclosed shortly.

First, after another dicey wartime sea voyage we arrived at the port of Halifax in Nova Scotia. This reminds me of a hoary Canadian story: An English father sent a cable to his brother in Vancouver saying: 'Daughter Jane arrives Halifax noon Wednesday. Please meet.' The brother sent back the following: 'Why don't you meet her, you are nearer?'

From Halifax we went to New York and Washington where we clocked in with the British Army staff at the Embassy. It had been arranged for us to do an attachment to a US Army division in training before going to the Staff College. The Division was stationed in Baton Rouge in Louisiana in the deep south. We travelled in those days everywhere by train including very long distances. They were great fun being just as depicted in films and songs like *Chattanooga Junction*. We stayed at Camp Van Dorn with 63 US Division who were kindness itself but were not very interested in the war in Europe. We went on manoeuvres with them. As far as I could see all the Staff Officers at Headquarters, including the most senior ones, spent most of their time in putting together their equipment and cleaning their weapons and had very little time left for anything else.

We were not too far from New Orleans where we were able to spend a weekend. To me it was heaven to be in the historic birthplace of jazz particularly Basin Street, where I simply had to go. So after *Dinner at Antoine's* (literally) I took myself off there. It proved a little disappointing having been cleaned up for the sake of the health of 'soldier boys' and no longer jumping with jazz at dubious joints. However, on the corner of Basin Street and another street I heard the beat emanating from a cafe and on entering found a real swinging trio of piano, bass and drums. Having dined well, I was in a mellow mood and took over a microphone with a little opposition at first and even some enthusiasm later. It was indeed an ideal outfit to sing with and the repertoire inevitably included *Basin Street Blues*.

I should now explain that our luggage had been lost in transit and had not yet caught up with us and we only had uniform to wear everywhere, so I would suggest that happily I am the only British Army Officer to sing *Basin Street* in Basin Street wearing His Majesty's uniform. I did not tell His Majesty as I fear he might have been displeased without knowing the full circumstances, but I like to think that it did a little for Anglo-US relations. After two weeks in Louisiana we proceeded via St Louis to Kansas City. Leavenworth is some thirty miles away and better known throughout the States for its prison rather than its army base.

The Command and General Staff School had to cope with large numbers of potential staff officers in their rapidly expanding army, including Air Force officers who were then part of the Army. There were nearly 1,000 students, many of whom had very little military experience. For example, I sat next to a full colonel who was a civilian judge destined for the Army's legal department; as he had no knowledge of tactics and the like he was very grateful for the help I could give him.

By our standards the instruction was very elementary and also intensely dull. The lecturers would repeat to us word for word the official military manual which we had been told to study the night before. If they deviated by so much as a comma I am told they were reprimanded. We all spent much of the time in a large hall listening to such monologues and never went out on exercises. It became very dull and tedious; so much so that one volunteered to go to the dentist in order to get a break. This was allowed, and American dentists are very good.

There was one excitement to interrupt the tedium. Every now and then, without warning, at the end of the period question papers were rapidly distributed and had to be answered on the spot. The questions took the now common form of putting crosses in boxes to questions such as: 'Would you attack the enemy on the right flank, left flank or centre?' Probably no sensible officer would have attacked the position at all and the number of experienced US Army officers, ex-West Pointers, said so. This was a mistake and I swallowed my pride and military instincts and put the 'x' where I thought teacher wanted it. I scored well at this and at half-term it was announced that I was the top student. This, the Commandant declared, was a disgrace to the US Army officers and they must do better. Presumably they did because I never heard at the end of term where I had been finally placed. But it was the first time I had been top of anything.

Work was very hard and the days long. Occasionally they were enlivened by a presentation by the British Army Colonel on the Staff, sometimes assisted by we British students. It is easy to be critical but at this time, as I have said, it was necessary to turn out staff officers with some sort of basic training in large numbers as quickly as possible. Much of the course has been changed since then, with our exchange of views and many of our methods incorporated into US Army staff training. But I speak as I found it in 1945. One aspect of the United States Army staff work which never ceased to amaze me was the vast amount of duplication and red tape involved. Everything had to be checked and double-checked before a decision could be made; also every staff post was at least duplicated with one chap watching the other, possibly necessary in the American way of life.

As I have said, I was surprised by the amount of red tape, far more than in the British Army. But there was one big difference between us. A commanding general, *eg* a divisional commander, with guts, could cut through the red tape with comparative ease and scatter it aside. As we all know, British red tape created by the Civil Service is more like iron chains which can only be severed very rarely with great difficulty, even by someone like the Chief of the General Staff.

After an intensive week's work we did get a short break at the weekend which we spent mostly in Kansas City where we were made members of the officers' and business men's clubs. It was a big place in a dry State but another jazz scene, different from that in New Orleans. I enjoyed some splendid bands, and the most memorable occasion was hearing Lionel Hampton's band in full swing at a Palais de Dance. There I met a young US Air Corps officer and his girlfriend who showed me around the town the next day and invited me to their family to share their Thanksgiving dinner: a charming occasion and typical of American generous hospitality.

One trip is worthy of mention. About a hundred miles north of Leavenworth lies the old township of St Joseph which was the starting place for the early Oregon Trail. We went there by train and booked in at a hotel on the Saturday night. Having signed in, we had not long been in our room when two very fierce gentlemen in unmistakable police plain clothes burst in, followed by the manager bearing the register: 'You goddamn Limeys are ribbing us,' he said. 'No one can have these names.' Now my companion rejoiced in the name of Lord Guildford and had signed 'Guildford, Lord, Major'. I had entered 'Crook, Major'. This had been too much for them, but on presenting our identity cards we managed to persuade them that these really were our names. After this we became great pals and the plain clothes cops took us round St Joseph, showed us the nightime scene, and it developed into a great evening.

I naturally gravitated towards the few regular soldiers amongst the students, with whom we had more in common. An illustration of how quickly the United States Army was expanded is shown by the following story. One of my friends was a West Point officer who had come to the course straight from Italy after commanding an infantry battalion there and in North Africa and had had a pretty sticky time. He was greatly relieved to be ordered home to the course and so be able to be reunited with his wife. It was not until the course had ended that he heaved a sigh of relief and disclosed that he had been on one previously. He was cunning enough not to do particularly well because he was afraid he might be found out and sent back.

The course came to an end early in the New Year and one was given a handsome diploma as evidence that one had graduated from the United States Army Command and General Staff School's Infantry Course. After reporting to the British staff in Washington, we were invited to visit the United States Army Military Academy at West Point, *ie* their Sandhurst. I had decided to go there via Chicago where I had some contacts. There my kind hosts took me to a smart hotel where we saw and heard Cab Calloway and his band. On the way back to their home in a taxi we passed an area which they said was the 'Loop' and was a place to be avoided as being very rough and seamy. So I promptly took myself back there after saying goodnight. It was indeed a pretty lurid area but there was inevitably some splendid music. Here, as elsewhere in both UK and USA, soldiers in uniform were treated with great kindness and allowed to sing should they be tiresome enough to want to do so. If the accompaniment was right I could barely resist it. I was wearing an officer's British Army greatcoat and, after rendering a few numbers, returned to the bar where I was greeted with a pat on the back and the comment: 'Say, buddy, that was great. Are you a Marine or something?' This was perhaps the biggest compliment I could have and the height of my fame. So it was no problem when luckily I met up with the great Louis Armstrong and he genially allowed me to render a vocal chorus with him. Once again I think it was *Dinah*.

West Point is about fifty miles up the River Hudson, north of New York. This was a truly lovely spot and we were again treated with the utmost courtesy and were most impressed, especially by the strictness and discipline. An illustration of this which has always stayed in my mind took place at mealtimes. The junior cadet at a table of approximately a dozen fellow cadets fetched and served the food for the others. Then he sat strictly to attention and did not touch his own meal opposite him until given a nod by the senior cadet at the table. Frequently it seemed that he had only seconds in which to dispose of it. Perhaps it is not surprising that some senior US Army officers suffer from ulcers. But we greatly enjoyed our visit to West Point and had the cheek to consider it a much better military academy than Leavenworth.

We then hung around New York waiting for a ship to take us back to the UK. This enabled me to visit several jazz joints and hear amongst others the immortal Art Tatum. We eventually embarked on the *Louis Pasteur*, a French passenger liner. She was a fast ship and this time my sea journey passed quickly without sight or sound of the enemy; but she was so unstable that it seemed that if one walked from one side to the other she rolled with you; I have never been a good sailor.

9

R.A.P.W.I.

The earth is full of anger – Rudyard Kipling

A posting to the Far East soon came through and I was sent off to the war there, as anticipated by General 'Bubbles' Barker, having been elevated to wartime lieutenant colonel.

It seemed that there was some urgency for my presence out there as I was included as one of the passengers on an Imperial Airways flying boat. The rest of my fellow travellers were civilians of some significance. The pilot was the famous Captain Jones, a very experienced and senior pilot: this was just as well, as he had to find a suitable piece of water on which to land some eight times between Poole Harbour and the river Hoogli, Calcutta. We eventually arrived there during a monsoon storm. My companions were met and whisked off to dry homes and beds whilst I was left stranded, as no one knew anything about me. I somehow made my way to Calcutta soaked through and managed to secure a share of a room in the Grand Hotel. This was mainly due to my cap badge, the White Horse of Kent. I basked in the reflected glory of our 4th Battalion who had put up such a magnificent show in the defence of Kohima. My room-mate turned out to be Dougal Young, a highly entertaining individual whom I had known at Cambridge.

Eventually I reached the Headquarters of Allied Land Forces South East Asia (ALFSEA) at Barrackpore, outside Calcutta. The drive out was quite an experience along a route crammed with the traffic of India, bullock carts, ramshackle buses, overladen trucks, mad taxi drivers and army transport. I observed that the driver of the army vehicle was often a soldier from West Africa who had been made to wear army boots since leaving there, which he hated and it certainly did not improve his driving.

For a while I was bandied around HQ ALFSEA where the senior 'Q' staff officer turned out to be Jimmy Riddell, formerly my Company Commander in Karachi, now a Major-General. He found me a job in charge of the newly constituted RAPWI Control Staff. 'RAPWI' stood for Recovery of Allied Prisoners and Internees. I was hoping for an operational job and viewed this appointment with some dismay at first but it turned out to be the most exciting, demanding and worthwhile assignment I ever had.

We had to start from scratch and the initial planning involved me in journeys to headquarters throughout India from Calcutta to Delhi, Bombay, Poona, Secunderabad and Madras as well as Kandy in the hills of Ceylon which housed the Headquarters of the Supreme Commander South East Asia, Admiral Lord Louis Mountbatten. I travelled in various forms of transport – jeeps, trains, trucks and a motley collection of aircraft. I well remember one particularly hair-raising flight from Madras to Bombay during a storm in an Indian Airways plane piloted by an Indian. To this day I don't know how he managed to land us right side up.

I eventually became based in Bombay at the Headquarters of 34 Indian Corps where the planning for Operation Zipper, the invasion of Malaya, was taking place, and my small unit was included in the landing tables. The idea was for the small RAPWI team to land in the later stages of the invasion, make its way to the camps, and improvise from there. We were to act as specialist advisors to the Commanders in the field who had to carry out the actual evacuation of the POWs. It has to be stressed that the conditions for the recovery of POWs in the Far East were very different from those in North-West Europe. There by the time the POW camps were reached there was full administrative backing for an Army Group with all the medical, welfare and other facilities. Whereas in South East Asia there were only Indian Army Formations with very limited resources.

But one day, 14 August to be exact, whilst in the air I heard the wonderful news that Japan had surrendered as a result of the dropping of the 'H' bombs. To digress: it has become fashionable to deplore the use of nuclear weapons against the 'poor' Japanese. It cannot be emphasised too strongly that this action saved untold suffering and hundreds of thousands of Allied lives. Certainly there would not have been any prisoners left to recover, as the Japs had issued orders that they should all be killed before they could be rescued. True there were Jap casualties, but these would have been many more if Japan had been bombarded and invaded. No, without those two bombs I and many, many others would not be here to tell the tale.

But to return: the Japanese surrender caused an immediate and sweeping change of plans for RAPWI. No longer was it just Malaya but the whole of an expanded South-East Command to include extra territories just added. The number of POWs and internees still alive in SEAC could only be guessed at but the total was thought to be over 100,000. Figures for Singapore were estimated at around 20,000 to include 6,700 Australians, 4,000 Indians and 3,000 civilians.

We hastily put together teams for Siam, Indo-China, Hong Kong, Java and Sumatra and I elected to go to Singapore. This meant attaching myself to 5 Indian Division who were destined to land there. So I got myself to Rangoon, where I disgraced myself by falling down a scrambling net while joining an assault ship. This damaged my back for which I was to pay dearly later.

We arrived off Singapore at dawn on 5 September. Although they had been ordered to surrender by their masters in Japan no one quite knew what the soldiers on the spot would do, so the invasion was to be carried out in phases according to a careful plan. But I had one objective – Changi Gaol at the other end of the island from the port, and could not wait for two days for troops to reach there.

I got ashore quite early and on the docks came across a British prisoner of war who had been working there. He was a bright chap who commandeered a car from a Chinese banker. He drove us out to Changi through Jap troops and I was the first person to reach the prison camp. There I met the senior British officers, Lieutenant Colonels in their late 40s looking far older after their long ordeal in prison camps. As a young Lieutenant Colonel of 30, I looked and felt like someone from outer space. They took me to a smart bungalow where we found the Jap Commander, a General Saito. From him I demanded instant and complete obedience to my orders which he accepted without demur.

They bade me to a formal lunch which, although very sparse, was made into quite an occasion; the menu was illustrated with camp scenes by Ronald Searle. During lunch someone said: 'Will you talk to the chaps and tell them what's happening?' 'Of course,' I said, without thinking. I was taken to one of the towers of the gaol, where surprisingly they had managed to set up a microphone. Below in a square was a sea of worn, sickly faces belonging to emaciated scarecrows gazing expectantly up at me. I was greatly moved and it was one of the most frightening moments of my life, though there was no danger. I managed to pull myself together and tell them about the landing and when they could expect to be properly rescued and evacuated.

There were going to be tremendous problems. The relieving force was an Indian Division at assault scales with no luxuries and Indian type rations. Ships and their stores had had to be arranged at very short notice. When they did arrive there were difficulties in unloading them; this had been done under the Japs by POWs who were no longer available and the locals were reluctant to come forward at first. Thus a crisis soon arose over feeding the ex-POWs. I represented this to the Commander of the Force, General Mansergh, who promptly saved the situation by ordering his troops to go on half rations, thus sharing what there was. The Royal Navy, too, came up trumps by producing fresh bread every day.

But all this was to come. Meanwhile I left them in very good heart at Changi and returned alone to the safety of the British lines in Singapore. I made my way to the Goodwood Park Hotel where my staff had established the Headquarters of No 2 RAPWI Control Staff in accordance with the plan.

My staff consisted of four British officers and four Indian officers plus a few clerks and drivers. All of them were to work exceptionally hard and achieve remarkable results. In addition, I had a medical team commanded by Jerry Hayes, a magnificent Devonian who was to prove a tower of strength and a tremendous help to me both personally and professionally. My 2i/c, Ronnie Somerville, took charge of organising all the supplies, stores, rations and transport. This was appropriate as he was to become a Deputy Quarter Master General in the Ministry of Defence, a Major-General. Meanwhile he did much of the detailed work, allowing me to fight battles at top level on behalf of the ex-POWs.

One of the captains, Peter Pearce Gould, a tireless worker, took on the duties of an adjutant, dealing with all the paper work. He organised an Information Bureau in conjunction with the Red Cross which was inundated with queries and performed a most important task. We had tremendous support and help from Red Cross teams who worked side by side with us. There was also a small party from the YWCA who were a great help in dealing with women and children.

I also had a Platoon of FANYS (First Aid Nursing Yeomanry) attached, an assortment of very high grade young ladies who could and did turn their hand to anything from running the reception of POWs at the Raffles Hotel to the job of my Personal Assistant, most efficiently performed by the charming Patricia Kirrage. Technically they were drivers and I had to be very sweet to their boss, Mrs Curry, when she arrived in Singapore to justify their misemployment. But when she saw how much good they were doing she was very understanding and allowed them to continue.

Many difficult problems confronted us, the health, feeding, documentation and repatriation of what turned out to be some 30,000 POWs and internees. In addition to Changi there were three other camps on the Island and a civilian camp for internees at Sime Road. The first few days were very worrying and we lurched from crisis to crisis. Funnily enough, health was not the worst as might be expected. The British Military Hospital was found to be in good usable condition. The medical stores had hardly been touched by the Japanese during their years of occupation as they did not consider a sick soldier worth bothering about if he could not fight. This explains their total disregard for the health of POWs who in their eyes should not be alive anyway. Torture by the Kempetai had been brutal and terrible.

But initially obtaining and distributing adequate supplies was very difficult. I have already mentioned that owing to problems in the docks we had to go on half rations. Another example was when the ship bringing NAAFI stores eventually arrived, the first crates which were unloaded were found to contain boxes of booze whilst what we really needed were basic things like soap, toothpaste, and writing paper. My small staff had to deal with many unforseen but significant distractions such as finding the Bishop of Singapore, J.L. Wilson, and giving him a message from the Archbishop of Canterbury. There were other distinguished people who had suffered terribly at the hands of the Japs and had to be treated with tact and understanding.

One evening, at the end of a very difficult conference, I was handed a signal saying that Lady Edwina Mountbatten was arriving to see the conditions of the RAPWI. 'Oh Lord,' I thought, 'this is the last straw. I have enough on my plate without wasting time on a lady whom I have vaguely heard of as a rich, pampered playgirl.' I felt she would be a flaming nuisance. How wrong I was!

She came to Goodwood Park the next morning, escorted by a staff officer and Major-General Telfer Smollet, Chief Medical Officer. She was very charming and promptly won me over by saying 'Colonel, I know you are very busy and don't want to take up your time. Could you please provide me with a guide to take me round the camps, and I will see you later.' So I took her at her word and did just that. She came to my evening conference and sat quietly while people discussed developments and problems. At the end she said: 'I have seen for myself what the situation is and admire very much all that you are doing under very difficult conditions. Now what can I do to help? What do you need most?' 'Knives, forks and spoons, soap, towels and certain medical stores,' I replied. 'Right, let's see what can be done: first we must make a list.' And with her staff officers she helped to do this. Then she competently dictated a signal to SEAC 'Personal for Dickie (Mountbatten) am sending my plane to collect vital stores for RAPWI. Please ensure immediate provision and despatch.' Then we sent a less 'personal' signal with the list. It was a most efficient performance by the gracious, high-powered lady. And sure enough they all turned up two days later. In addition she did immense good amongst those still in camps and hospitals. Her charm, genuine sympathy and understanding, together with her air of competence, won over all whom she encountered and raised morale. She was of tremendous value and I became her devoted admirer. She also visited many other places in South-East Asia, often at great danger to herself, and later I was to accompany her around the Netherlands East Indies.

Admiral Mountbatten came for the Surrender Ceremony which he had carefully planned. It took place in the Council Chamber of the Municipal Buildings and I was privileged to be present along with some ex-POWs and internees for whom I had obtained places. I am the proud possessor of a unique photograph showing the Japanese Commander in the act of signing under the stern eyes of the Supremo, flanked by his Allied Senior Commanders. My photo, too, is signed, by Admiral Mountbatten in one corner and by the Japanese Area Commander in the other. The latter was General Itagaki as the overall Japanese Commander, Field Marshal Teruchi, was certified sick at the time. (He was made to surrender in person later.)

Lord Louis also visited Changi where he was greeted with some suspicion and even antagonism at first. Understandably they felt he might have arrived sooner after the dropping of the bombs on Japan. However, he jumped on a box and addressed them in his inimitable style. He made no apologies but told them what was going on in the world and explained why he had not been able to get to them earlier. By the end, he had completely won them over and they would have fought another war against the Japanese with him if he had asked them to.

Only four days after the landing, Pat Kirrage and I had the satisfying experience of seeing off two ships, one of them a Hospital ship, returning with ex-POWs to India. But for other destinations it was rather more difficult. The Movements people worked wonders and produced shipping from all over the place. In three weeks we had got away all those who were in Singapore when we landed and wanted to go. This was pretty good really, but to someone who had to wait up to twenty days it seemed an eternity. This earned RAPWI the rather unkind and unjustified title of 'Retain All Prisoners of War Indefinitely'.

There were over 6,000 Australian POWs in Singapore which I viewed with some trepidation as I feared they might be troublesome. Happily, I established a good relationship with their dynamic Commander Lieutenant-Colonel 'Black Jack' Gallegher who could keep them under control. We found a pleasant area by the sea which they could occupy while waiting for repatriation. Fortunately this did not take long, as shipping was quickly produced to take them home. In fact by the time a large Australian repatriation team under a Brigadier arrived they had all left.

So after three weeks a great deal had been achieved in repatriating the Singapore RAPWI but a new situation arose causing serious problems. RAPWI started arriving in Singapore from the terrible camps in Indonesia and Sarawak. It was just acceptable for the RAPWI in Singapore to remain in their camps until they could get on a ship, but it was totally unacceptable to expect RAPWI rescued from one awful camp to go into another one on arrival in Singapore, especially the infamous Changi. So I had to find somewhere decent for them and took over the Raffles and Seaview Hotels. Admittedly they were the best, but in my view nothing was too good for these unfortunate people who had suffered so much for three-and-a-half years. But this view was not shared by the Civil Affairs people who wanted to restore these hotels to commercial use. I had to fight my case right up to the top.

I vividly recall the scene on the airfield at dawn where I had gone to put my case in person to senior Commanders. I did so first to the Army Commander, who just shrugged his shoulders and walked away. I then approached the Supremo himself who listened sympathetically and ruled in my favour. Thus people who had endured and survived the most appalling conditions did come back to something civilised.

Throughout I had the Supremo's support and backing. This was just as well as I did not have it at all levels. In my capacity as the top representative of the RAPWI I had to have dealings with senior officers. It is perhaps interesting, if impertinent, to retail my impressions of these distinguished men. They were people who had won battles but I can only speak as I found them in my unusual role. Admirals Power and Morse were always sympathetic and helpful but it was easier for them. General Slim was mainly concerned about the Indian Army ex-POWs and not interested in others. General Dempsey did not appear to be interested. Major-General Hone, Chief Civil Affairs Officer, was more concerned with restoring the fortunes of the returning business community rather than those of the imprisoned internees. Maj-Gen Mansergh, the Commander of the soldiers on the ground, was magnificent, always sympathetic and helpful where he could be.

We continued to be very busy with no two days or problems the same. Embarkation dates and times kept on being changed; unexpected new arrivals landed at the airfield: the sick in hospital and those who stayed behind needed understanding and advice – 'counselling' it would be called now; there were countless queries about the whereabouts of people 'last seen . . .'. There were many visitors who had to be briefed and shown round. One of these was Gracie Fields who arrived quite early to give concerts. She was of great value and I had fun one evening escorting her round the Happy World, a Chinese Fun Fair. And who should turn up but Jumbo Courtney, complete with penny whistle. He had managed to get himself over from Borneo where, with a gang of local thugs, he had been headhunting Japanese. He stayed nearly a week and we had some 'jam sessions' and visited all the joints. It was great to see him again.

At the end of October we gave a party to celebrate the repatriation of our 50,000th RAPWI. Among a number of distinguished guests we were honoured by the presence of Lord Louis and Lady Edwina Mountbatten. It was quite a party in spite of, or perhaps because of, the gin which was of Indian make, being all that was available. It was terrible stuff but could just be disguised in a fruit cup.

By mid-November the fugitives arriving from outside Singapore had reduced to a trickle and we had sent most of them back to UK. There were a few who did not want to leave despite medical advice, which gave rise to tricky problems. Ships were no longer freely available and changes in their sailing dates caused some complaints and difficulties. In addition, there was the ever present problem of the unfortunate Dutch of whom some 15,000 remained in Singapore as there was nowhere else for them to go. They mainly administered themselves and were well organised but they were still a concern of the RAPWI Control Staff.

Nevertheless the main task in Singapore had been accomplished and I was ordered to move on.

10

Netherlands East Indies

We're dyin' in the wilderness the same as the Israelites – Rudyard Kipling

Around the time of the Japanese surrender, the Netherlands East Indies, later to become Indonesia, were added to South-East Asia Command. Accurate information about the situation in the islands under Japanese rule was scanty. The Dutch assured us that all that had to be done was to put them back and they would take over control and carry on as before the Japanese invasion. This was far from the true state of affairs. The Indonesians had seen all their Dutch rulers removed and humiliated and they had no intention of having them back. They are tough people who had become quite well organised militarily with Japanese training and equipment.

So on returning we were confronted by strong opposition and only attempted to establish footholds in the main ports, Batavia, Semarang and Sourabaya in Java, Medan, Padang and Palembang in Sumatra. This required a reinforced Corps, 15 Indian Corps, which became Allied Forces Netherlands East Indies or AFNEI. The problems confronting the British – operational, administrative and political – were formidable. Whatever we tried to do was wrong in somebody's eyes. If we supported the Dutch, our European wartime Allies, we were indicted by the 'anti colonialists' including America and even Australia. If we supported the Indonesians we were very strongly criticised by the Dutch as letting them down; also this was not popular at home when some cases of Indonesian atrocities became known and in particular the murder of a British Brigadier in Sourabaya whilst touring the city with a moderate Indonesia leader trying to arrange a truce.

RAWPI Control teams, and Lady Mountbatten, had preceded the main Force and succeeded in evacuating the British from appalling camps to Singapore, as we have seen. The Indonesian leaders, who were entirely hostile to the Dutch administration, were at first prepared to accept the RAPWI organisation which became in effect the only form of local administration for a time. Any inhabitants of NEI who were in danger of losing their lives if they fell into the hands of the Indonesians were as far as possible given protection by us. Finally, a number of people who had not been imprisoned by the Japanese were interned under atrocious conditions by the Indonesians and they, too, became the concern of RAPWI. Thus at one time the total numbers in NEI for which the RAPWI organisation was catering amounted to approximately 200,000.

It was into this cauldron that I stepped as it came to a boil at the beginning of December, dressed as a full colonel. I was to form and take charge of a new branch at HQ AFNEI created by the Brigadier Administration, the ebullient Alastair Maclean, called RAPWI COORD. Its task was to co-ordinate the RAPWI activities in NEI, organise the recovery of the internees and to act as a liaison between the Allied Commanders and the civil authorities, both Dutch and Indonesian. It was in effect a Civil Affairs Branch.

I took with me the reliable and hardworking Peter Pearce Gould who coped admirably with the office work. I was fortunate enough to be allocated a most competent English speaking Dutch lady, Mrs Esme Buurman, as secretary. The Dutch side of the branch was made up of an Air Force Colonel, his staff officer and lady secretary. The Colonel was a magnificent chap, Dick Asjes, a distinguished aviator who fought gallantly with the RAF and was awarded a Distinguished Flying Cross. Full of energy and vigour, he commanded respect and attention wherever he went. Although representing the Dutch point of view he could always see things from the Allied viewpoint as well and was most co-operative and totally loyal. We got on extremely well together and became firm friends which has lasted until this day. He brought with him a Mitchell Bomber which was to be used by us as a transport plane and proved invaluable.

My role was to take some of the strain off senior officers by meeting with and at least listening to the East Indies leaders. I dealt with the Governor General, Dr Van Mook, a most reasonable man who got little support or understanding from Holland. The senior military man, Admiral Helfrich, was most intransigent, advocating all-out war against the Indonesians. He was replaced by General Spoor who proved more amenable and controlled his firebrands. I was also to have dealings with the Indonesian leaders, Soekarno and Sjahrir who were hated and reviled by the Dutch as collaborators with the Japanese.

I was fortunate in serving under two outstanding Force Commanders, first Lieutenant-General Sir Philip Christison, and later Lieutenant-General Sir Montague Stopford who was a friend of my father and had been the Commandant of the Staff College when I was there.

But my immediate task was to deal with the problems of Semarang. Some way inland from the port, the Japanese had set up camps for 10,000 Europeans, including women and children. There were no immediate means of getting them all away and as time went by the Indonesians started attacking them at night and stealing and murdering. A Battalion of Gurkhas had to be sent to rescue them and they were now temporarily located in Semarang, which itself was under siege.

Dick Asjes and I made strenuous efforts to find somewhere for them to go and some means of getting them there. We managed to get ships diverted and produced from all over the place. During December some 20,000 were evacuated. Only about 1,000 could go to Holland but the majority had to remain within South-East Command. This meant that in the end we sent 12,000 to Singapore, 5,000 to Ceylon and 2,000 to Bangkok. We were very conscious that these were human beings who had already suffered a great deal but at least we managed to save their lives.

I had to get around and visit these unfortunate people in their camps. There were a number in and around Batavia which was protected by a Brigade under command of an airborne officer, Pat Western. Our Mitchell plane took us to Sourabaya where 5 Indian Division were virtually at war suffering only too many casualties. They were still commanded by my old friend in Singapore, General Mansergh, who was as helpful as ever. We also flew to Semarang where a curious situation prevailed. The Parachute Brigade under Ken Darling was considered to have insufficient troops to guarantee the safety of the town so a Japanese Battalion was allowed to keep its arms and assist. Of course they did it very well!

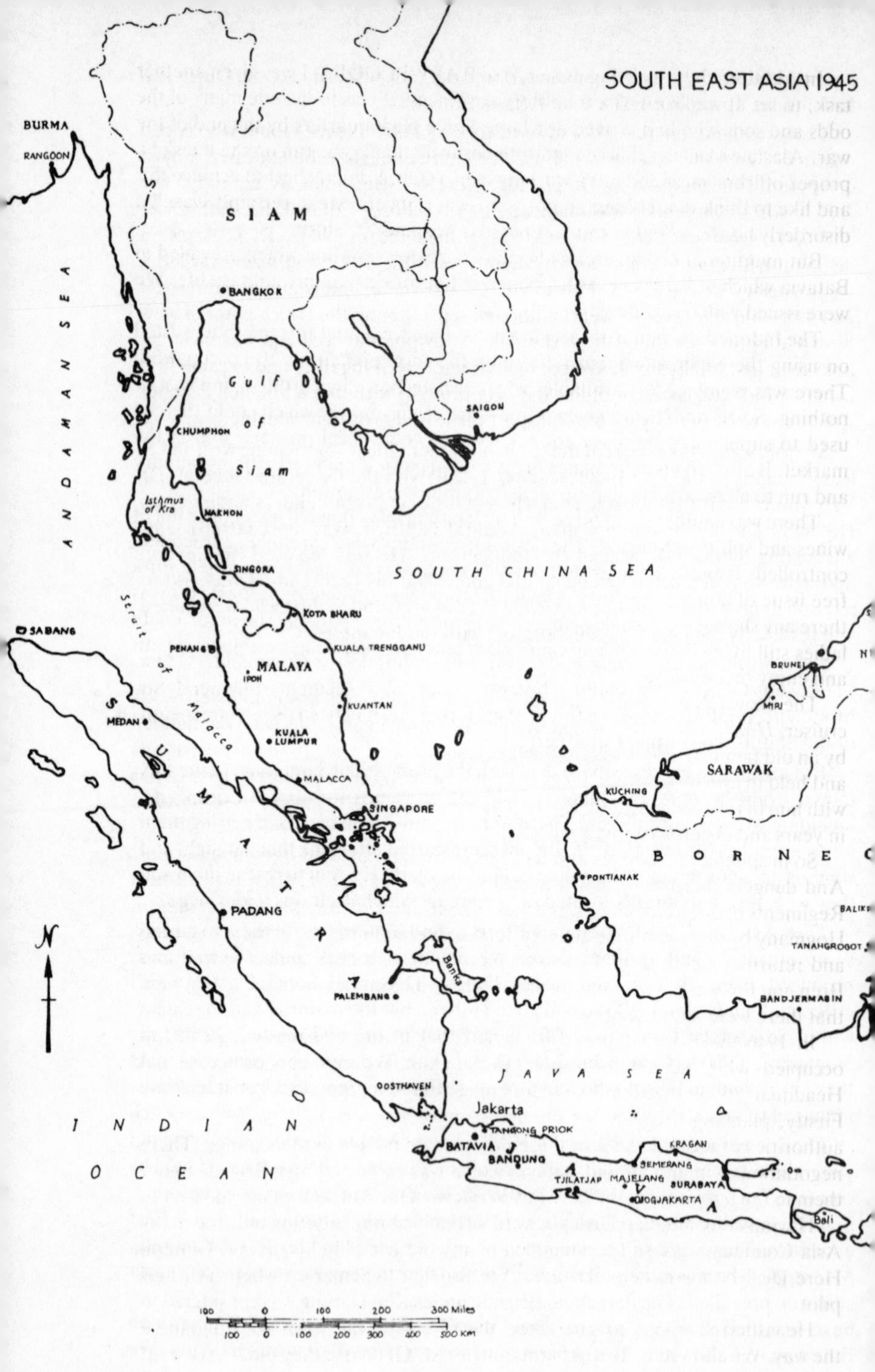
SOUTH EAST ASIA 1945
BURMA
RANGOON
SIAM
ANDAMAN SEA
BANGKOK
Gulf of Siam
CHUMPHON
SAIGON
Isthmus of Kra
NAKHON
SINGORA
SOUTH CHINA SEA
SABANG
Strait of Malacca
KOTA BHARU
PENANG
KUALA TRENGGANU
MALAYA
IPOH
MEDAN
KUANTAN
KUALA LUMPUR
SUMATRA
MALACCA
SINGAPORE
BRUNEI
MIRI
SARAWAK
KUCHING
PONTIANAK
PADANG
Banka
TANAHGROGOT
BANDJERMASIN
PALEMBANG
JAVA SEA
OOSTHAVEN
Jakarta
TANGONG PRIOK
BATAVIA
BANDUNG
KRAGAN
SEMERANG
TJILATJAP
MAJELANG
SURABAYA
JOGJAKARTA
JAVA
Bali
INDIAN OCEAN
N
100 0 100 200 300 Miles
100 0 100 200 300 400 500 KM

In addition to the exacting demands of RAPWI COORD I was given another task, to set up and supervise a new officers' mess. It was to include many of the odds and sods who had arrived at a large Force Headquarters by the end of the war. Alastair Maclean charged me with ensuring that it was run on the lines of a proper officers' mess and not a working men's club. I did my best to achieve this and like to think that H Mess, if not a pre-war Officers' Mess, certainly wasn't a disorderly house. Whether this was popular was another story.

But mention of messing reminds me of a unique situation which prevailed in Batavia which sadly has never happened before or since in my military life. We were issued with free money!

The Indonesians would not accept the old Dutch colonial currency but insisted on using the paper money introduced by the Japanese during the occupation. There was plenty of this available, which was technically worthless and cost us nothing. So all ranks were given a free issue of this money which could then be used to supplement the basic rations with excellent local produce sold in the market. It also left enough change in my case to pay a servant, pay for my laundry and run to an occasional slap-up meal in a Chinese restaurant.

There was another splendid perk: The Japs had left a bonded warehouse full of wines and spirits untouched. The desirable contents were carefully guarded and controlled. Issues were made to bona fide applicants. A mess could indent for a free issue of booze for a party. Obviously there were plenty of parties! Nor was there any shortage of female company to escort to these parties. The unfortunate ladies still living in the Tjideng camp were only too pleased to be able to get out and enjoy themselves.

The Royal Navy, too, were their usual helpful and hospitable selves. A cruiser, *HMS Sussex*, was in support of us and often in port. She was commanded by an old family friend, Captain Edward Cooper. Ted was a friend of my parents and held in awe by me when I was a small boy. Now it was strange to be on a par with him in rank and position. But he was extremely nice to me and the difference in years and experience forgotten.

So in spite of the dangers and indifferent climate, life had its compensations. And dangers there were, not the least on New Year's Eve when two Scottish Regiments of different outlook and make-up decided to settle their differences on Hogmany by demonstrating actively. The action included the firing of weapons, and returning home from a party on New Year's morning amidst indiscrimate Bren gun fire was a hazardous business. Though I must admit that I do not recall that there were any casualties.

In 1946 the British officers in the RAPWI Control Teams were still fully occupied with the administration of the camps under our protection. At Headquarters, in addition, we were concerned with two main considerations. Firstly, planning and carrying out the handing over to the responsible Dutch authorities concerned of the ad hoc RAPWI organisation. Secondly, carrying out negotiations with Indonesian leaders to obtain the release of the RAPWI held by them in the interior. All the British had of course been evacuated long before.

Having dispersed large numbers of Dutch RAPWI throughout South-East Asia Command, it was necessary to go and visit them and try to raise morale. Here Dick Asjes was wonderful both as an inspiring person and as a proficient pilot.

He visited Singapore several times, usually calling in on places in Sumatra on the way. We also visited Bangkok, which from my point of view was great fun. We took Pat Western with us nominally as second pilot. He was a champion 'swanner'. We were accommodated in the best hotel free and treated like royalty by the Siamese who, under pressure, had sided with the Japs and so were technically defeated enemy at this time. The royal touch included attending the races in the same box as some charming princesses. I backed a funny looking outsider who won me an agreeable number of taels (pronounced 'tickles'). Exploring Bangkok at virtually no expense was a delightful experience.

Dick Asjes did most of the work and had a hard time trying to explain to Dutch military personnel why they could not go back to Netherlands East Indies in uniform. (Explanation anti-colonial opinion led by the United States of America.)

We also visited the Dutch RAPWI in Ceylon. The journey was quite an adventure. First we flew to Sabang, a tiny island off the northern tip of Sumatra, where we could refuel at a Dutch naval base. Then we proceeded non-stop across the Indian Ocean to Colombo in Ceylon, a flight of over 1,200 miles over the sea in a twin-engined wartime plane taking nearly six hours. My Air Force friends thought we were mad. Dick's navigation was spot on, which was just as well. It was comparatively easy to hit Ceylon on the way out. But if we had missed the little island of Sabang on the way back we would have been left with no place to go and very little fuel with which to do it.

The evacuated Dutch had been sent to Kandy up in the hills. It had been the Headquarters of Admiral Mountbatten and South-East Asia Command but they had nearly all gone and the empty messes and hutted accommodation made a reasonably pleasant place in which the evacuees could stay. But it was a long way from anywhere and was only temporary, as naturally they were longing to be settled at home. Dick and I flew up to the old airstrip at Kandy and visited all the camps. At least we could show them that they were not forgotten, thus making our hazardous journey worthwhile.

11

Venture into the Interior

These grateful acts,
Those thousand decencies, that daily flow
From all her words and actions
John Milton

Lady Louis Mountbatten paid a return visit to the camps in Java which she had first toured shortly after seeing me in Singapore. I had the pleasure of escorting her and it was a fascinating experience. Women who had had to remain in camps for a further six months after three-and-a-half years under Japanese tyranny can hardly be expected to enthuse about the visit of another woman who was in no way incarcerated anywhere. Yet they did. Lady Mountbatten, in her inimitable way, won over the hearts and raised the morale of all she met. She was regarded with genuine affection and admiration by these unfortunate Dutch ladies and her visit was a talking point for many a dreary day to come.

We were used to travelling around under difficult and sometimes dangerous conditions. I had had several very dicey flights but our return trip from Sourabaya back to Batavia was the most hair-raising I had known. We ran into a tremendous tropical storm forcing us to bump along in turbulence just above the jungle tree tops amidst blinding rain, thunder and lightning with no visibility. The only passenger who was quite unconcerned was Lady Louis. The rest of us were terrified.

However, we made it and the next day flew up to Bandoeng. This was a large, pleasant hill station away from the steamy heat of Batavia below. It was occupied and protected by us because it contained many European families threatened by the Indonesians. It was defended by 23 Indian Division under command of Maj-Gen Hawthorne. The journey by road through the hills was dangerous and convoys were often attacked.

A Wing-Commander Tull had done a first-class job in the name of RAPWI in looking after the needs of the APWI. Lady Mountbatten was very impressed with what he had achieved and was also relieved to find that conditions had improved greatly everywhere under our administration. In addition to Tom Tull, there were a number of officers who did stirling work to help the APWI in each of the places which we occupied throughout Netherlands East Indies. They were in effect Civil Affairs administrators and were much appreciated by the locals. But they were unsung heroes; though recommendations were put forward by the grateful Dutch for awards by their Government, politics intervened and our Labour Government did not allow us to accept them.

Nevertheless the unhappy Dutch families had to remain in camps while the world debated the rights and wrongs of the conflicting cases of the colonial Dutch and the native Indonesians. It should be pointed out that numbers of the Dutch had lived in the East Indies for generations and had no home in Holland. Many were known to be held by the Indonesians in the interior of Java under grim conditions. All this time we were negotiating with the Indonesians to get these people out. There were also still many Japanese to be evacuated.

These negotiations were a delicate business and progressed very slowly. To move things along it was decided to risk sending in a small military mission into Indonesian-held territory to discuss matters with their 'Government'. The mission consisted of Brigadier Ian Lauder the Brigadier General Staff, myself RAPWI COORD, and Lieutenant-Colonel Laurens Van der Post, Political Advisor. The latter after being released from imprisonment by the Japanese remained at his own request because of his knowledge of the conditions in Java and his sincere desire to help bring about peace.

We set off at dawn in the Force Commander's Dakota accompanied by Dr Sjahrir, the Indonesian 'Prime Minister', and flew inland to an airstrip near the town of Solo. We were met by a motley collection of 'soldiers' in various uniforms and carrying a variety of weapons from wooden spears to tommy guns, who constituted a guard of honour. A short car drive took us to Solo station where a large crowd had gathered. The train was a pleasant surprise. We were given an air-conditioned parlour with hot coffee and later an excellent breakfast in the dining car. After an agreeable journey we reached Djogdjakarta, the Indonesian capital.

There we were whisked off to meet 'President' Soekarno. Taller than the average Indonesian, he commanded their respect but was not a pleasant character. But he was polite and wished our mission well. Next we went to the 'War Office' where our real work began and we held a conference with the heads of the Armed Services and Police, presided over by the Minister of Defence, Sjarifoedin, a Christian Sumatran who, by his personality, managed to keep in check the Javanese Mohammedans.

The object of the conference was, as already indicated, to arrange the evacuation of the Japs and prisoners and internees (APWI). We were surprised and pleased to find they were anxious to get rid of them and to help us as much as possible. Their difficulty was to evolve a plan which they could sell to their more extreme elements. After two laborious sessions we managed to arrive at some sort of solution.

The next problem for the Indonesians was where we should spend the night. They were obviously worried about us. They first offered us a bungalow in the hills, but later cancelled this, no doubt for safety reasons. It transpired that the local hotel formerly called Grand Hotel but now Hotel Merdeka was full of refugees from Bandoeng and that feelings were running high.

However, after some delay the three of us were given one room from which someone had been turfed out. Two armed youths of the student type sat on our veranda as guards. Ian Lauder and I wrote up our notes while Laurens Van der Post chatted to the guards, unfortunately in Dutch.

Fortunately I had brought a bottle of whiskey, so fortified by this we went into the dining room for dinner. The two guards sat at the same table with us and continued to talk in Dutch. In the dining room were a number of young men in various uniforms bristling with weapons. It became very evident that they did not appreciate our presence at all. In spite of increasingly threatening noises we finished our meal – which was very good – and returned to the solace of our whiskey, much to the relief of our guards, one of whom immediately disappeared.

He returned in about twenty minutes with a truck full of reinforcements including his Company Commander and a nasty bit of work who called himself Chief of Police. They said they were sorry that there had been some trouble. We replied with true British phlegm that we didn't know there had been any. However, they increased our local guards, posted more at the entrances to the hotel, and the Chief of Police remained with us. He was a fervent communist who spoke English and had been in charge at Magelang, which meant in effect that he was proud of having helped to murder a number of helpless women and children.

What with the guard on the veranda, barbed wire being erected at the window and entrances and hostile noises coming from outside, one realised how much one was a complete prisoner at the mercy of these people. However, when the bottle was empty we went to bed in the right frame of mind and slept soundly; but I was glad to see that dawn. We were given a good breakfast but not allowed to move from the room. We found out that the armed young men in the dining room had just come from fighting around Bandoeng and naturally resented us. 'Why are the enemy in our midst?' they asked. They were told that this was an English peace mission, but were not satisfied as they had heard Dutch being spoken and so we must be Dutch. They were assured that we were not, but insisted on knowing our names. My good American surname upset no one, but Van der Post was very nearly the last straw. Apparently it was a very close thing.

Our hosts were anxious that there should not be a repetition of what happened to the 'other Brigadier' (the murder of Brigadier Mallaby in Sourabaya), a sentiment which we heartily endorsed. But to be fair, they looked after us effectively and, after a satisfactory final conference, we returned to Batavia by the same complicated way by which we had come involving cars, train and aircraft. We took with us some of the Indonesian negotiators so that we could clear up any points after reporting to General Stopford.

Things began to move quite soon and the first trainload of APWI reached Batavia about the time the Supremo, Admiral Mountbatten, paid a farewell visit. It is worthy of note that all of them were evacuated before the British left the East Indies, thanked by no one.

My task with RAPWI COORD had come to an end and it was time for me to take off my Colonel's red tabs before I got used to them. So it was decided that I should take up the appointment of General Staff Officer Grade 1 at HQ 23 Indian Division in Bandoeng with General Hawthorne. I was pleased as, in spite of the undoubted excitements of the RAPWI world, I would be doing something orthodox and operational.

But it was not to be. On my last trip to Sumatra in the Mitchell with Dick Asjes, I was suddenly smitten with the most excruciating pain in my back. The flight back from Medan to Batavia was a nightmare. I was admitted to hospital and it was diagnosed as sciatica, a hangover from the scrambling net in Rangoon which has plagued me to this day. After a spell in hospital I was just able to walk and Dick arranged for me to be flown home in a KLM four-engined passenger plane. This was very gracious of the Dutch as otherwise I should have had to get to Singapore somehow and then languish in a hospital ship.

The journey by KLM was not uneventful. First we went to Bangkok where I was looked after by Ronnie Somerville, now a Lieutenant-Colonel. After painful stops at Calcutta, Karachi and Basra we staggered into Cairo with engine trouble. This meant a delay while it was fixed, and we were put into the fashionable Heliopolis Palace Hotel. I was in no state to enjoy it, which was a pity as King

Farouk gave a huge party there with food, fireworks, dancing girls, the lot. We eventually arrived at Schipol, the airport for Amsterdam, and were greeted by large crowds cheering and waving Union Jacks. I thought it was nice of them to make such a fuss but that they need not have bothered. It turned out that a plane bringing Winston Churchill had just touched down on another runway!

I was met and looked after by a delightful Dutch family whom I had befriended in Batavia. They managed to get me a seat on another Dutch plane to London. When I reported my presence to the War Office they seemed to be taken somewhat by surprise.

12
Lessons

Our business like every other, is to be learned only by practice and experience; and our experience is to be got in war, not at reviews – Sir John Moore

On return to UK the sciatica was examined by several members of the medical profession trying to avoid cutting me open; but the excruciating pain struck again and I did not care whether they cut my head off. Instead they cut out a lumbar disc, *ie* a laminectomy operation, one of the early ones. It was performed by a brilliant surgeon, Mr R.H. Young of St George's to whom I am ever grateful. Although I have suffered a fair amount of back trouble over the years, I am a pretty good advertisement, having become fully fit and commanded a company in the jungles of Malaya and a parachute battalion in action.

In order to be able to have post-operational treatment at St George's Hospital I had to go to the War Office. I was posted to the Training Directorate which was then located in the Horse Guards. This was nice, as one window of the office looked out on the front courtyard where the Cavalry changed the Guard every day. The other window looked across Whitehall and we had a front row seat for State and Royal processions, including the wedding of Her Royal Highness Princess Elizabeth and Prince Philip.

Our department, Tactical Investigation, was responsible for the promulgation throughout the Army of training doctrine, including its collation, editing and publishing and for some subjects actual production; the work was very interesting and worthwhile. The Director of Military Training was Major-General Sir Charles Keightley to whom I reported direct on some subjects.

General Keightley is perhaps less well known than some more flamboyant generals. Yet his record is unique. No one has had more practical experience of the art of command. He spent nearly all the war commanding men in action from a Regiment to a Corps. A cavalryman, he commanded an infantry division as well as armoured formations. After the war he commanded the British Army of the Rhine, was Commander-in-Chief Far East Land Forces, and finally Commander-in-Chief in the Middle East where he commanded all the Allied Forces at Suez for which he is probably best remembered, which is a shame as it was not a success through no fault of his, but of the politicians.

A brilliant, courageous leader, he was always most unassuming, modest, considerate, courteous and kind. He did not push himself forward or ride roughshod over others (or write a book!) which is perhaps why he never became a household name. He was a great teacher and to hear him on the art of command was a revelation. I was fortunate indeed to work for him, first in London and later closely in Singapore and Cyprus.

It was during this time at the War Office that perhaps the seeds of authorship were sown. I was the founder/editor of the British Army's own magazine. It was then called the *British Army Journal*, later renamed *British Army Review*, and has developed into an excellent publication under the direction of some distinguished editors.

As part of my writing exploits I 'ghosted' some items for senior officers and even, in conjunction with General Keightley, produced a revised version the 'Principles of War' which met with the approval of the CIGS Field-Marshal Montgomery. I also wrote an article called 'The Atomic Bomb – what every officer should know'. In it I concluded that the best defence against the atomic bomb is not to be there when it goes off! In 1947 this was not quite as silly as it sounds now. Anyway, the article aroused some interest and was published in two commercial, military magazines as well as our free *British Army Journal*.

Another of my jobs was to do all the administration for Monty's annual exercise at the Staff College. It was a great occasion attended by all the Services hierarchy from all over the world. The production of the exercise was done by a special team under a Brigadier. I just did the background stuff in co-operation with the admirable Camberley staff to make sure everyone was comfortable. Amongst many items was the provision of cars for all these dignitaries in the days when transport was in short supply. One very senior officer, who shall be nameless, was awarded the decoration 'MTF' by the ATS drivers (Must Touch Flesh).

So my time as a 'Whitehall Warrior' went by as my back recovered and I was passed A1 again. I was posted to the Staff College and from trying to record the lessons of the war, went to trying to teach them. On the strength of this I wrote what I considered to be a good article – 'The Lessons of War, Why Bother?' – postulating that military training pamphlets were not tablets of stone officially directing us to prepare for the last war. It was not true then and I trust is not so now. The 'tablets of stone' were used by Moses to record the Ten Commandments which have survived in spite of doubts and sneers. Likewise the Commandments of War – the Principles of War – also survive.

As a member of the Directing staff I doubt if I have ever worked harder in my life. I was allocated to the Division at Minley Manor where I had been a student. As I have said earlier, the Manor is a replica of a French château situated in woods some three miles south-east of Camberley. It had lovely gardens and a first-class cricket ground set amidst the rhododendrons. The pitch was lovingly tended by the groundsman, Mr Dallimore, and was the subject of much favourable comment by first-class batsmen. Now it is the tar macadam parade ground of the Sappers. Progress or desecration?

The lucky ones at Minley were inclined to refer to going to Camberley as 'going slumming'. This improper attitude is illustrated by the following incident.

I arrived at Minley for the last term of the course as an observer to get the form before starting in earnest with a new course next year. Postings were known and the atmosphere was pretty lighthearted by then. For reasons which escaped me there was a feeling prevalent that the Royal Navy and consequently the Army DS at Minley had in some fashion been insulted by some people at the RMA Sandhurst. Quite how this had come about I never discovered, but the feeling was definitely there; so much so that after an end-of-term party, prompted by the Navy representative, it was decided that some positive action was called for to register our displeasure. A party of us set off for Sandhurst in the dead of a December night. There we removed one of the old cannons and manhauled it back to Minley. It was quite a business and as we struggled over the bridge at

Blackwater we aroused the interest of the local bobby. However, he was assured by our Gunner leader that it was 'the Royal Foot Artillery moving station' and went on his way satisfied. We parked the piece on the lawn outside the Manor and there it was at dawn for all to see with a notice saying that it had been 'presented to the Staff College Minley Wing by the Qualifiers of the 6th Royal Naval Staff Course'.

Realistically it was not a very good idea and a fair amount of umbrage was taken. We were lucky that there were two very broad-minded Commandants at Sandhurst and Camberley, blessed with a sense of humour, in the shape of Generals Hughie Stockwell and Dudley Ward respectively. Apologies were made, the cannon returned, and nothing more was said. In retrospect I think we were very leniently treated.

The pressure of work on a DS with a syndicate of ten was very high indeed. Certainly in the summer I saw in a number of dawns as I laboured away correcting the students' offerings. But this made time for sport which in my new found fitness I greatly enjoyed. I played for the Staff College hockey side which was pretty good in those days and had a first-class fixture list including some top civilian clubs. I became secretary and enjoyed it very much.

But the standard of cricket was even higher and it was a club cricket at its best. I am proud to have been a member of the 1949 side which is considered to have been one of the best ever seen at the Staff College. We played 20, won 16, drew 3 and lost one, absurdly enough against the Butterflies. Dougie Dalgleish of the Leicesters made an admirable captain and Alan Waldron of the Hampshires took a record number of wickets. I made some good scores and caught the most catches. Next year was not so successful either for myself or the team.

Most of the students had had active experience and many were pretty high grade. All had something to contribute and it was often hard to keep up with them, much less one move ahead. In fact several of them were destined to reach the very top of the Army. But I will only mention one. He was not from the British Army. One of my best friends at the US Army Staff School at Fort Leavenworth was Lieutenant-Colonel Bill Yarborough who had commanded airborne units. We had kept in touch and at Christmas 1949 I received a card from him saying 'I have been posted to a place called Camberley, do you know anything about it?' To which I could reply: 'Yes, indeed I do, I am there.' So our friendship was renewed and blossomed during his year at Camberley. He was a genuine admirer of the British Army, and our Airborne Forces in particular. In the States he organised 'Green Berets' on the lines of our Red Berets and SAS, and became a Lieutenant-General.

The Directing Staff, too, contained some distinguished and remarkable characters. Again I will only mention one. Lieutenant-Colonel Peter Moore, RE, known as 'Streak' because of his very long and thin figure, was a splendid character. He had a very fine war record in which he didn't care a damn for the enemy. He continued the same attitude in peacetime and rarely gave a damn for anyone, yet was not offensive. With a sharp wit and wicked sense of humour he was a stimulating colleague and livened up life in the DS library. He had an old Bentley Tourer in which we used to drive on DS recces where we usually shared a bottle of champagne and giggled in the back row during the otherwise solemn proceedings. He left the Army shortly after Camberley and went into television. Sadly he died young and was a great loss.

We studied the campaigns of the great military commanders of the past. Doing some research on the Peninsular War in order to impress my students, I came across a splendid piece of 'Wellingtonia' which I have always treasured. It is an extract from a letter written by the Duke of Wellington from Spain about 1810:

To the Secretary of State for War, Lord Bradford
My Lord,
If I attempt to answer the mass of futile correspondence that surrounds me, I should be debarred from all serious business of campaigning.

I must remind your Lordship – fo· the last time – that so long as I retain an independent position, I shall see that no officer under my command is debarred by attending the futile drivelling of more quill driving in your Lordship's office – from attending to his first duty – which is, and always has been so to train the private men under his command that they may, without question, beat any force opposed to them in the field.

I am, My Lord,
your obedient Servant,
(sgd) WELLINGTON

One of the highlights of the Staff College year was the Battlefield Tour which was great fun but jolly hard work for the DS. One had to know the 'pink' *ie* the solution exactly, and could not make it up as in academic exercises. The first year we did the battles along and across the Rhine in 1945. We lived in a train which was well stocked and comfortable, an agreeable state of affairs in those austere days. We visited the scene of the airborne landings across the Rhine and returned via Arnhem. The next year we studied the Normandy landings both by sea and air and stayed in the Lycée Malherbe at Caen where an entire Division of sixty students could be fitted into one of its dormitories. The plumbing was not so capacious. We crossed the Channel from Portsmouth to Cherbourg and back aboard a destroyer, *HMS Contest*, to whom we presented a Camberley Owl in gratitude for their hospitality.

After supervising a syndicate for several terms one was given a term off which was known as 'swinging'. This had nothing to do with my kind of music and was not as jolly as it sounds, as one was charged with rewriting precis, in my case Infantry, and producing an exercise on a phase of war. I drew the Withdrawal, the most difficult and depressing. Exercise Lion was the much cursed result of my efforts. One good thing came out of it. While doing a recce of Horsedown Common whence we withdrew, I observed a house on a ridge at the back end of Fleet which was obviously in a desirable position. I went back and found part of a large house for sale of which we eventually took possession.

During all this there was little time or opportunity for jazz activities at a microphone which was probably just as well. But I did arrange with my good friend Chappie D'Amarto of Hatchetts to bring a small swinging band to the Minley Ball with whom I performed till dawn. People didn't mind as it meant the music went on longer.

It was time to be a doer rather than a teacher. So I was pleased to be posted back to my Regiment and to join the 1st Battalion at Shorncliffe about to leave for Malaya even though it meant dressing as a Major after nearly six years as a Colonel of one sort or another (the last two years at the Staff College being local and unpaid).

13

Malayan Emergency

The Jungle is Neutral – E. Spencer Chapman

It was a grey, gloomy dawn in February when some 600 officers and men of the First Battalion the Queen's Own Royal West Kent Regiment, 1 RWK, mustered to take a special train from Shorncliffe Camp, Folkestone, to Liverpool. We were not taking families with us as accommodation was very limited in Malaya, but Peter Buckle had found somewhere for Angela and Sarah.

Among those seeing us off was Joan, widow of 'Swifty' Howlett and mother of Geoffrey who had just joined the Battalion from Sandhurst. She came up to me and kindly said 'Paul, I'm so glad Geoffrey has been posted to your Company. Please look after him for me.' Well I like to think I did, as this gangling, green young subaltern saw action with me in Malaya and Egypt and developed into an outstanding leader of men shown by the rank and appointments he held when he graciously wrote the Foreword to this book.

We embarked on His Majesty's Troopship *Devonshire* and ran into very rough weather in the Bay of Biscay. Something went wrong in the engine room and we had to heave to in a severe storm, pitching and rolling to an alarming degree; most things were battened down but a piano ran amuck in the lounge. Willie Spurr, with whom I was sharing a cabin, and I strapped ourselves into our bunks and clung on for dear life. It was not much fun but one had not reached the final stage of sea sickness (first you are afraid that you are going to die, then you are afraid you are not) when the OC Troops, a Wing-Commander, came on the ship's public address system and in an obviously panic-stricken voice announced 'there's no need to panic, the Captain and crew have everything in hand and will be able to save the ship. We are not sinking!' I don't think anyone had even contemplated this until he made this unfortunate announcement which had the reverse effect of what was required. But the engineers did a very fine job of repairing the damage under appalling conditions and we made a collection for them when it was all over.

But the excitements on our month-long voyage were by no means over. The conditions on a troopship for officers while not exactly those of a luxury liner were not too bad, but for the soldiers were pretty grim. They just had a space for their hammock in the crowded lower decks where things were miserable in cold weather and horrible in hot. When we reached Port Said we were flying the Plague 'Keep Off' flag because it was thought we had a case of smallpox on board. We had not, but no one was allowed ashore and we all had to be vaccinated by local doctors with blunt needles. Again no one was allowed ashore at Aden and as we steamed away on a moonlit night there was a cry of 'Man Overboard'! The Ship stopped and turned round to look for him. Meanwhile everyone had to be accounted for which took time. Eventually nobody was found to be missing and we proceeded on our way to Colombo where we were at last able to go ashore after being cooped up together for twenty-three days.

The soldiers in my Company were mostly National Servicemen who, after completing their recruit training, had some eighteen months left to do overseas. This meant that we could train and operate together virtually unchanged for quite a while which was good. I was twice to have National Servicemen under my command on active service conditions and found them jolly good. In my unfashionable opinion it was a pity the Regular Army was so anxious and ready to give up conscription.

At last the *Devonshire* deposited us in Singapore and we spent a month in transit in the barracks at Nee Soon, scene of an infamous incident during the Japanese occupation. The Battalion was under the competent and kindly command of Tony Martyn with butterfly chaser 'Crocus' Andrews as 2/ic and the rumbustious Dicky Dover as Adjutant.

My Company underwent three weeks' concentrated jungle training very well organised by the Jungle Warfare School in Johore Bahr. It was as good an introduction to life in the jungle as could be managed in the short time available but we were to find that we still had a lot to learn.

The Battalion's role was to provide security in the north of the State of Selangor and the south of Perak and it was based on Kuala Kubu Bahru (KKB) at the junction of the main road north to Ipoh and the road east across the mountains to Bentong. My Company was to go on some thirty miles north to a small place called Trolak, where we took over a company base in a rubber estate from Right Flank Scots Guards (dare I repeat it, but I find a note in my diary that the place was dirty and unhygienic). At this time the Chinese Communist terrorists (CTs) were very active and were trying to drive the European settlers out. They were doing pretty well and life for a planter was precarious and frightening, especially for the wives. Most stuck it out bravely and one admired them but they did reap their rewards as the price for rubber and tin was very high.

We lived amidst the buildings of a rubber estate belonging to a Mr and Mrs Browne who were very kind to us and helped to make us reasonably comfortable. It wasn't too bad, though the smell of fomenting rubber was always with us and pretty pungent at times. We were in the Tanjong Malim District where there was an excellent Police Officer in charge called Ian Henry. We worked closely together but he could not supply me with much accurate information about the CTs.

I did not believe in sitting back waiting for something to happen but tried to seek them out. This meant that there was always someone out on patrol or ambush. In the absence of specific information I used the famous book by Spencer Chapman, *The Jungle is Neutral*, as a bible and guide. In it he tells how he survived three-and-a-half years behind the Japanese lines living in the jungle, often in camps with Chinese gangs. There were some of these camps in our area around the Slim river. I thought it a good idea for patrols to try and find these camps in the hope that the Chinese terrorists might be using them again. Nothing ever came of it and it became a bit of a sick joke with the soldiers. But it was good training and was to stand us in good stead later on. For we were finding that the Malayan jungle which is rather a mysterious and alarming place at first really is neutral and not hostile as some jungles in other parts of the world are. For example, there are no dangerous animals and one hardly ever sees any. The worst creatures by far were bloodsucking leeches which suddenly appeared out of nowhere, rather like flies in the desert. Happily snakes were few and far between but I once shot a hissing Cobra in the head with a single shot from my revolver, which raised my image with the soldiers no end!

As well as the Brownes we made friends with other planters in our area and I'm happy to say that none came to any harm during our three months there. A Sunday curry lunch was a pretty dangerous event.

After three months we moved back to Battalion Headquarters at KKB. Here, although we had an operational area of our own, we were under the not very friendly eye of the Regimental Sergeant Major. Rightly he tried to keep up a decent standard of regimental soldiering in such matters as drill, which I hated as much as my soldiers. I managed to organise things that we were nearly always out on operations when threatened with a Battalion parade. We had some successes in killing a few bandits which helped to justify this.

At least while at HQ I was able to organise and captain our cricket side. We had some very good players, including two members of the Kent County ground staff as well as Rex Shearburn and Dicky Dover. I also played for Selangor and the Army Malaya. People thought that playing cricket was a bit of a scrounge but I can honestly say that I found a long day in the field in the sun more exhausting than a quiet patrol in the depths of the jungle.

Just before we left KKB we took part in an operation near Kuala Selangor on the coast in mangrove swamps. Unlike the jungle these are full of nasty creatures and wading through them was horrid. Geoffrey Howlett's platoon had been left at KKB in case there were any emergencies. And an emergency there certainly was.

The High Commissioner, Sir Henry Gurney, and Lady Gurney sometimes took a break away from the steamy heat of Kuala Lumpur in the pleasant, cool hill station of Frasers Hill. This meant a drive along the road east, past KKB, which included many twists and bends as one climbed upwards through the forest which came right down to the roadside. There were many good places for an ambush. But there had not been one until Saturday, 6 October 1951, when Sir Henry and Lady Gurney were murdered in their car in spite of having an armoured car escort.

We got back to camp from the swamps in the evening tired and dirty anticipating a wash and a drink to find that Geoffrey and his platoon had rushed off up to the scene of the ambush and we were to follow as soon as possible. There was just time to issue 48 hours' rations but we had never operated high up in the hills before and, coming straight from sea level, did not think to take any warm clothing. Even in the tropics there is quite a difference between 0 feet and 4,000 feet as we were to find out. So off we dashed to meet Geoffrey at the scene of the murder. He showed me the terrorists' ambush positions and their tracks leading up into the forest. By now Geoffrey had become very skilful in following tracks, working in conjunction with a native tracker. The forest here is very thick and one can see absolutely nothing at night. So we had to wait till dawn before we could set off to follow these tracks. As a result it transpired that we were always twelve hours behind the terrorists. It was apparent that there were quite a lot of them, well armed, and they could not be treated lightly.

At dawn we climbed upwards into the thick forest and after a while Geoffrey reported finding a large camp near a stream which had recently been occupied. This was greeted with excitement and spurred us on to redouble our efforts. We were to find two more but there was never anyone there.

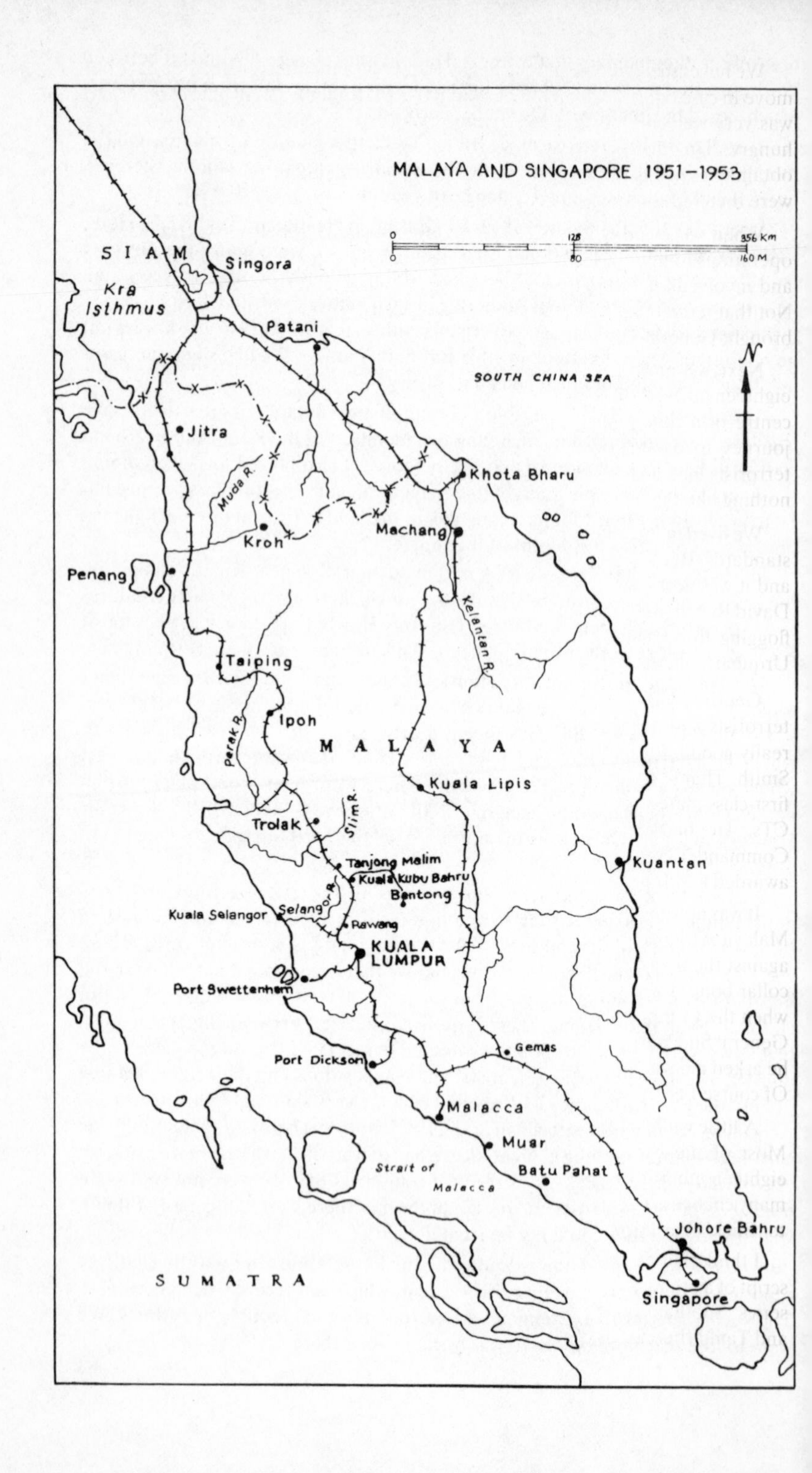
MALAYA AND SINGAPORE 1951–1953
0
128
256 Km
0
80
160 M
N
SIAM
Singora
Kra
Isthmus
Patani
SOUTH CHINA SEA
Jitra
Muda R.
Kroh
Khota Bharu
Machang
Penang
Kelantan R.
Taiping
Ipoh
Perak R.
MALAYA
Kuala Lipis
Trolak
Slim R.
Tanjong Malim
Kuala Kubu Bahru
Bentong
Kuantan
Kuala Selangor
Selangor R.
Rawang
KUALA
LUMPUR
Port Swettenham
Gemas
Port Dickson
Malacca
Muar
Batu Pahat
Strait of
Malacca
Johore Bahru
Singapore
SUMATRA

We never saw the sky, and the nights were long and bitterly cold. One dare not move in case one got lost in the blackout. The dawn took a long time coming and was very welcome. As the days went by our rations ran out and we were very hungry. On the last evening there was only curry powder left. Water was obtainable though it meant a long trek to the stream in the valley to fetch it. We were then reduced virtually to currying our boots to make a hot drink.

When we eventually emerged from the jungle it was to discover that the operations to find the murderers had moved further on into the forest-clad hills and involved a large number of troops and planes. But they didn't catch them. Not that it did them any good, as in place of Sir Henry as High Commissioner it brought General Templer who was to defeat them.

Next we moved south and took over a company base at Rawang about eighteen miles north of Kuala Lumpur (KL). Rawang was a busy place, being the centre of a tin-mining area as well as rubber and palm oil estates. The short journey to KL involved going through a steep pass in the forest where the terrorists had carried out several successful ambushes. We made sure that nothing like that happened in our time.

We lived in the buildings of a disused tin mine which was pretty civilised by our standards. Because of this and our proximity to KL we were liable to have visitors and it was necessary to be prepared for them. This suited one of the subalterns, David Reoch, a charming young man who much preferred being polite in camp to flogging through the jungle. Among the visitors was the GOC General Roy Urquhart, and we had the author Graham Greene to tea one day.

Geoffrey Howlett, on the other hand, genuinely liked operating against the terrorists and did it increasingly well. We were greatly helped by getting some really good information from an excellent plain-clothes police officer called Bill Smith. Thanks to him we had several successes against the CTs, culminating in a first-class platoon action efficiently led by Geoffrey resulting in the killing of five CTs. He had developed into a courageous, skilful and inspiring Platoon Commander and for this and several other actions against the enemy was awarded a Military Cross.

It was now the hockey season and I played for the Battalion and the Army. The Malaya Army side went down to Singapore to play in a triangular tournament against them and Hong Kong. In the match against Hong Kong I dislocated my collar bone. I was watching our match against Singapore with my arm in a sling when the Commander-in-Chief, my former boss in the War Office, Lieutenant-General Sir Charles Keightley came and spoke to me. To my surprise and delight he asked me whether I would like to come and be his Military Assistant at GHQ. Of course I accepted and left it with him to fix the posting.

A little while later the Company went to Penang Island for rest and retraining. Most of the National Servicemen with whom I had lived and operated for eighteen months were now due for repatriation home. So there were about to be many changes. Thus it was without many regrets that I handed over the Company to 'Blick' Waring and took off for Singapore for a very different role and scene.

I think that this period in Malaya can best be summed up by reproducing the script of a broadcast I gave in KL one Saturday night on Radio Malaya as part of a series 'Spotlight on the Emergency'. It was also transmitted in Malay, Chinese and Tamil (but not by me!).

ANNOUNCER: The spotlight this week turns on the jungle itself and shows some of the problems which must be faced by soldiers on the ground. It is given to you by Major Paul Crook, Commander of 'C' Company, Royal West Kents:

'Sometimes when I come to Kuala Lumpur, my friends pull my leg and say: 'You're slipping, Paul. How did your people manage to miss those bandits last week?' Well, fair enough. But underlying the humour, that is really a very serious question. How *did* we manage to miss those bandits? As Company Commander I *ought* to know. And when I get the answer, it's my job to see that we don't miss those bandits next time, if that is humanly possible.

'My own Company has recently had successes. We received information and we killed bandits. Once or twice we have been very lucky. But there have been times when we wondered if we should ever kill a bandit again. So let me answer this question: Why don't we kill more bandits than we do?

'Firstly, go into the jungle and look round. Try and find any spot where you can ambush ten bandits and be sure of killing them. You won't find it. A bridge over a stream is an ideal place. But even with a gang of twenty bandits, there will never be more than three bandits on that bridge at one time. The rest, at the first crack of a rifle, will be into cover like lightning.

'So that is my first point. Bandits are trained to scatter and vanish. They have brought evasive action to a fine art. If they carry out their military drill properly and skilfully they should be able to get away. So should any soldier in the same circumstances. But, of course, our soldiers are trained to stand and fight and not to disappear. The bandits who do get killed are, more often than not, the careless, the under-nourished and the ill-trained. Naturally, there are exceptions, particularly in the case of individual bandits who, in ambush, make only a single target. But even so, you sometimes hear of individual bandits making their escape. He is there one moment. You open fire. The next moment he is gone. And you can hardly believe your eyes.

'This happened only a few days ago near the perimeter wire of Rawang Town. One of our patrols in ambush fired at a bandit from close range. He was hit three times, but nevertheless managed to force his way through thick barbed wire, cross a fast-flowing river and hide in a hut. Fortunately, that same night his presence in the hut was reported and that bandit was captured in a seriously wounded condition.

'Take Perasamy, No 2 Indian bandit to Manian, who was killed by one of our patrols a fortnight ago. A Bren gun opened up at him at 300 yards range and hit him but he sprinted uphill for another 200 yards. A grenade blew off the back of his head but he still ran on. It took yet another three bullets to finish him off. Although mortally wounded, Perasamy might easily have dived into the undergrowth and never been seen again. (And that would have been another bandit unaccounted for.)

'Now about camps. Sometimes on the News you hear that a bandit camp was surrounded. Twelve bandits were in the camp. Eleven got away. Why? To answer that we must take a closer look at the word 'surrounded'. In the jungle it is a theatrical ideal, impossible to achieve in practice. The nearest soldiers can get to a camp without being heard is about 200 yards. In the jungle this is a considerable distance. I have been led to a camp in jungle which was a meeting place for couriers and occupied for some time by twenty bandits. Yet it was quite impossible to see this camp until I was within twenty yards of it. There was only one approach route. A sentry posted on this only about 100 yards out could give all the bandits ample warning to get away in the jungle. The fact is that bandits have learned how to site their camps properly: some are near the jungle edge with the best possible cover for retreat; others are placed at the top of a steep slope. Under these conditions surprise is extremely difficult, especially when bandit sentries are fully alert, which they usually are. However, in spite of these difficulties bandit camps are attacked and bandits killed.

'Other difficulties which are not generally understood arise in the actual process of getting information from a surrendered bandit or informer. The problem is how to get an informer's ideas onto a map, and then transfer them from the map onto a spot in the jungle – which spot must be 100% accurate. Incidentally, the maps themselves are not always right.

'Surrendered bandits often know the position of their own camp well enough but have difficulty in locating other camps which they know to exist. A single wrong direction can jeopardise a whole operation; and a single word misunderstood in translation can spoil a promising patrol.

'Before closing, I must pay a tribute to the chaps who are doing this particular job for you. In my own Company, they are mostly young National Servicemen from the outskirts of London. It is remarkable to me how quickly they have adapted themselves efficiently to jungle life with cheerful good humour. That they have the right spirit is surely proved by the action of members of my Battalion who, although wounded and having lost their officers, fought off the bandits at Ulu Caledonian Estate without losing a single weapon.

'So there it is. There are many difficulties which arise the moment you step into the jungle, these *we* have to face. This we can do. But given your help and co-operation we can do an even better job.'

14
Singapore Again

Ship me somewhares east of Suez, where the best is like the worst, where there aren't no Ten Commandments an' a man can raise a thirst – Rudyard Kipling

The job of a Military Assistant to a Commander-in-Chief (MA to C-in-C) is unique; certainly there are not many of us. It is hard to define, as it depends primarily on the relationship of the holder of the appointment with his boss. I had a splendid boss, Lieutenant-General Sir Charles Keightley, and a very happy and successful relationship. The C-in-C had an ADC who looked after his social life and I took care of the rest. The aim was to make his working life as smooth as possible. In practice it meant controlling the bumph. I was authorised by the C-in-C to open absolutely everything addressed to him except for confidential letters from the Military Secretary because, as he said with a twinkle: 'If I'm going to be sacked, I should like to be the first to know.' Of course, he was not sacked but promoted to full General during my time.

I organised all the paper work that came to him, pruning some and adding a covering note to others as to their value and the need to read them carefully or quickly. The C-in-C would ask me to prepare a brief for him on some subject quite independent of anything submitted through normal staff channels. This was not always appreciated by the Chief of Staff. On my arrival he was the amiable Major-General Nigel Poet who did not seem to mind much but his successor the earnest Major-General Eric Sixsmith was not so amenable.

The mail included copied of telegrams and despatches sent by all the Ambassadors in the Far East. Most were beautifully written but very verbose and of little value except perhaps to the author's reputation in the Foreign Office. One only was brief and to the point. It was fascinating to meet these distinguished people when they came to Singapore for one reason or another.

But apart from matters of State there were two subjects which constantly exercised us and filled up two files, which I called 'Precedence' and 'What to Wear'. In Singapore at this time among the three Services there were at least five 2-star officers and three with three or more. That's quite a lot of stars on one small island, quite apart from visiting dignitaries weighed down with stars. The Governor of Singapore, Sir John Nicoll, as Her Majesty's representative, outranked everyone, whilst across the causeway the Commissioner General was the senior British citizen in the Far East. He was Ramsay Macdonald's brilliant son Malcolm Macdonald, and Willie Spurr of the Regiment was his MA which helped.

Etiquette and precedence were taken very seriously and when attending an official function all these people should arrive in strict order of precedence, *ie* the junior first and the senior last; woe betide the ADC who allowed his driver to get it wrong. This sounds simple enough but often led to arguments which required the tact and charm of my C-in-C in his capacity as Chairman of the Joint C-in-C's Committee to sort it out.

But worse and sillier still was the vexed question of what to wear at functions for which the dress was not stipulated. It would start with the ADCs at junior level agreeing but then someone would rock the boat, usually the Senior Service. Then it would be bandied around at MA level. Here the Royal Air Force and ourselves were at a disadvantage as the Royal Navy's counterpart to us was the Admiral's Secretary, a Captain, RN. Eventually all three C-in-Cs would ring each other up and at last it would be settled once again by Sir Charles's tact and courtesy. What a lot of fuss about nothing you will say, and you would be right but it certainly generated a lot of hot air in already steamy Singapore.

A major item was arranging the C-in-C's programme and visits. These varied from local units in Singapore to trips to Malaya and tours to Hong Kong via Siam and Indo China. Getting around was a problem as there were very few transport aircraft, for which we had to beg from the RAF. We could usually get a Valletta for Malaya but going further afield was much more difficult. The only aircraft capable of reaching Hong Kong was a converted York and that had to refuel on the way. It was the AOC-in-C's own plane which he naturally used often himself. So we had to book it when both the aircraft and its New Zealand pilot were available and serviceable.

I used to let the ADC go with him on visits to local units but tried to accompany him when going further afield. Thus when he went to consult with General Templer, High Commissioner of Malaya, I was able to call on my friends in the Regiment there. On visits to units I employed a simple ruse which gained my boss a lot of marks when he recognised a soldier who had served with him before whilst inspecting them. The trick was to arrange with the Adjutant that the soldier in question was, say, number three in the front rank and advise the C-in-C accordingly. Happily no Adjutant ever let me down.

The longer tours were not without incident. On one, when we were in Siam, my boss politely admired a very special 100-year-old egg and a dwarf tree in a pot. He was shaken to receive them as a gift, as is customary when one admired something in Siam. It was just as well that he had not admires one of the very attractive young ladies as I do not think the usually charming Lady Keightley would have been very amused. An adventure of a very different kind took place again en route to Hong Kong when we had to put down in Indo China at the port of Haiphong, at the mouth of the Red river, 100 miles from Hanoi. At this time the place was being run by the French, but only just, and it was under siege by the Viet Cong. We spent a disturbed night listening to the sounds of battle and were jolly glad to get away from it the next morning.

And there was the saga of the bird in Hong Kong. Once again the C-in-C had been given a present, a charming small bird which he thought Lady Keightley would like to have in Singapore. The problem was getting it there, especially as this time we were travelling on a civil aircraft. We were staying with the Commander British Forces Hong Kong, Lieutenant-General Sir Terence Airey. Just before we left for the airport it was decided to transfer the bird to a smaller cage to make it less conspicuous. This was to take place in Sir Terence's study but in the course of doing so, of course, Crook had to let it escape. We then had the edifying spectacle of two generals trying to recapture a small bird whilst I stood helplessly by (I hate fluttering things). Eventually they were successful and it was put into a small cage and covered over with newspaper so as not to draw attention to itself. I was charged with its care, losing it on pain of death. We embarked on the civil plane with me clutching this odd parcel which a suspicious stewardess could not persuade me to part with. I had to remain with it perched on my knee sometimes making strange noises, unable to leave my seat throughout a long and very uncomfortable flight. To my relief we got through Customs without trouble and the bird went to a happy home in Flagstaff House.

There was plenty of sport and opportunity to play it on the Island. I managed to get into the Army cricket side and not long after my arrival was looking forward to the match against my old friends from Malaya when I came out in a rash of large, nasty spots. At first I thought they were delayed jungle sores but on showing them to the Medical Officer there was much excitement and I was rushed off to the British Military Hospital. There I was kept in isolation for two days with suspected smallpox until it was diagnosed as chickenpox. This was absurd as I had already had chickenpox not once as normal, but twice. Secondly, chickenpox was one of the few diseases not endemic to Singapore. But chickenpox it was, in a way a great relief though it was not much fun being covered with spots from my feet to my eyelids in sweaty Singapore. It was thought the germ must have been carried by one of the children flying out from UK for the summer holidays and that I had caught it in the swimming pool at the Tanglin Club.

I recovered in time to play in the match against the Navy and take some wickets. It was rather droll that I played for Malaya as a batsman but now played for Singapore as a bowler. For a while I managed to get a fair number of wickets with my erratic leg breaks. I started a Free Forester fixture against the Singapore Club on the Padang and managed to collect just enough Foresters, including Brigadier Michael Green who had been an England tour manager in Australia and was now running the Selangor Golf Club. Geoffrey Howlett and Rex Shearburn came down from the Regiment to play as qualifiers. In the 'winter' there was some very good hockey and I also took up refereeing rugby seriously.

We had many important visitors but the most significant and charming was Her Royal Highness The Duchess of Kent. She stayed at Government House and, as Colonel-in-Chief of our Regiment, went to visit the Battalion in Malaya. Peter Buckle acted as her ADC.

Just before she left, the Keightleys gave a dinner party in her honour. Although the guests were the top brass it was to be informal for a change, dinner jackets not mess kit. When I arrived at Flagstaff House I asked the C-in-C if there was anything he wanted me to do. 'No, Paul,' he replied, 'the ADC can cope, just relax and enjoy yourself.'

I had arranged for an excellent pianist who led the band at Princes Restaurant to play for us instead of the usual military band. After dinner we were sitting out on the veranda while he played pleasantly in the background. Sir Charles took me up to talk to HRH and after a while said, 'Did you know, Ma'am, that Paul is a crooner?' and turning to me said, 'are you going to sing for us?' 'Of course not,' I replied, 'I couldn't possibly.' 'That's a pity,' continued Sir Charles, 'as he is an officer in your Regiment, Ma'am, couldn't you tell him to do so.' 'Oh yes, please do,' she said in her attractive, deep voice. 'There you are, Paul, go and see the pianist and get on with it.' So I was left with no option but to do as I was told. Fortunately I knew the pianist and he was a wonderful swingy accompanist. I like to think I was at my best and it certainly seemed to go down well with HRH; so much so that she accepted to accompany some of us to Princes, where the pianist continued playing with his band until the small hours. She obviously enjoyed this break from strict protocol though it caused some consternation in Government House.

I have said that my rendering of jazz numbers seemed to meet with approval but not by everyone. The next morning General Eric Sixsmith came storming into the office and said: 'If I'd known I was going to have to listen to that dreadful noise, I wouldn't have come.' I think he meant it, too. You can't win them all.

I felt I could add 'By Royal Appointment to my vocal credentials. (Incidentally I was not, and never have been, a 'crooner'.)

I tell this story not for my own gratification but as an example of Sir Charles's man management. If on my arrival he had told me he wanted me to sing I would probably have done one of two things; either left directly after dinner, or more likely drunk too much to help me though the ordeal. As it was, thanks to his thoughtful handling, I did neither.

Among a number of flights with the C-in-C one other is worthy of mention. One day the C-in-C and a number of senior staff officers from GHQ were going to a conference to HQ Malaya in Kuala Lumpur. At dawn we all got into the same plane, a twin-engined Valletta. After a while I felt very warm and, on looking out of the porthole, saw that flames were coming out of the engine on my side; soon it was very much on fire. The pilot announced that we would have to turn back and try to land on one engine; we had not quite reached the point of no return. So we flew slowly back getting hotter and hotter. As we circled over the airfield one could see blood waggons, crash vehicles and fire engines awaiting our landing, not an encouraging sight. However, we managed to touch down safely and rapidly evacuated the plane. It had been pretty alarming but no one was hurt. The RAF promptly arranged another aircraft, but here comes the anti-climax: all but one of the senior officers found pressing reasons why they must return to their offices at GHQ. The C-in-C thought nothing of it and just the three of us went to Kuala Lumpur after all.

Coronation year was celebrated in Singapore with parades, receptions, garden parties and balls, bringing the precedence files into action. Then General Keightley was appointed Commander-in-Chief Middle East Land Forces and a round of farewell visits had to be arranged and carried out. He left before his successor arrived and spent three days 'in limbo' on the journey. During this time I received signals for the C-in-C of both FARELF and MELF and felt I was dealing with the supervision of both Theatres on my own.

Ten days later the new C-in-C, Lieutenant-General Sir Charles Loewen, arrived with the CIGS and there was much to be done arranging their reception and programmes. I escorted the new C-in-C round his Command, involving the inevitable dawns at airfields. I managed to fit in a visit to the Regiment, who had now moved across the mountains to Bentong. I had a hair-raising flight back across them in an Auster to catch the C-in-C's plane at Kuala Lumpur.

Having handed over 'C' Company 1 RWK to 'Blick' Waring in Penang I now handed over Far East Land Forces to him in Singapore, *ie* he became my successor as MA to the C-in-C. Just before leaving I was appointed a Brevet Lieutenant-Colonel and posted back to the Battalion as second in command to Roddy Fyler, a most conscientious, competent and considerate CO.

I arrived back at Maidstone ahead of the Battalion and had the pleasant task or organising a visit by HRH The Duchess of Kent which brought me in touch with her again and her very pleasant and efficient secretary, Philip Hay. After a successful parade and march through Maidstone for a Civic Reception, the

Battalion went to Luneburgh in Germany. I had only just got there when to my surprise, delight and apprehension, I was posted to command a Parachute Battalion.

"Ready to Jump"
Parachute Regiment

MI'ILYA PALESTINE
L to R: Author, Peter Buckle. Background: 1938 Armoured Car.

TOURING WEST AFRICA
L to R: Author, civilian Pilot, General Sir George Giffard C-in-C, Captain John Giffard ADC.

WEST POINT
L to R: Majors Bircher, Grist, The Superintendent Major General F. B. Wilby, Author.

RAPWI COORD ALLIED FORCES NETHERLANDS EAST INDIES
L to R: Author, Esme Buurman-Buffart, Peter Pearce Gould, Jopie, Dick Asjes, B. L. Andries.

THE MINLEY FOOT ARTILLERY
The Troops had best remain anonymous.

RAWANG MALAYA
A Royal West Kent Patrol in a rubber estate.

TUNISIA CAMP CYPRUS
Leslie Leadbitter with an essential piece of equipment.

EMPLANING FOR CYPRUS
Dawn at Blacbushe: the Dog who was left behind.

JUNGLE WARFARE PANAMA
Patting the Puma.

SUEZ – EL GAMIL AIRFIELD 'P' HR + 5 MINUTES
Left: one of the barrels. Right: Control Tower. Background: Port Said.

SUEZ
The Air Contact Team. Background: captured Russian Tank.

THE JAMAICA DEFENCE BOARD
L to R: Mr Stuart, Secretary, Chief of Defence Staff, Prime Minister Sir Alexander Bustamante, Minister of Home Affairs Hon Roy Mcneill, Major Parker.

JAMAICA: VISIT BY U.N SECRETARY GENERAL
L to R: Major Green ADC, Author, U Thant, Lt Col Robinson CO 1JR.

JAMAICA: VISIT BY HER MAJESTY THE QUEEN MOTHER
L to R: ADC, Colonel David Smith, Her Majesty, Author, Jamaica Regimental Mascot and Handler.

HADRAMUT EAST ADEN PROTECTORATE
'Wedding Cake' Palace Seyun.

PRESENTATION OF NEW COLOURS TO 15th (SCOTTISH VOLUNTEER) BATTALION THE PARACHUTE REGIMENT
Colonel-in-Chief talking to Author and wife.

EL GAMIL 30th REUNION
L to R: Louis de Fouquières French cas evac pilot, C.O., François Collet French L.O., Gerald Mullins Adjutant, Stan Roe AOC Levant.

15
Parachuting

Knowledge Dispels Fear – Motto of the RAF Parachute Training School

'Hello,' I said, turning to the young man who had followed me in, 'I'm new here.' 'So am I,' he replied. And that's how I met Mike Walsh.

We were standing in the gloomy hall of the Officers' Mess of the Third Battalion, The Parachute Regiment, (3 Para) in Corunna Barracks, Aldershot. We entered a new world together. I had been a straightforward infantry soldier for nearly twenty years and was very proud of my Regiment. Now I was taking on a new one, a parachute battalion in the Parachute Regiment. Previously I had regarded the airborne world with a mixture of admiration, envy and even faint dislike. I was very soon to find out how very different, and in many ways far better, it was than the army I had known before. My West Kent soldiers were nearly all from the city and suburbia, solid, safe and comparatively easy to handle. The parachute soldier came from all over the United Kingdom seeking excitement, a volunteer who had found himself through parachuting and was a lively, restless but magnificent soldier.

So there we were in the Officers' Mess of 3 Para. But first we had to win our way there like any other parachute soldier.

Mercifully I was spared some of the horrors of 'P' Company as unfortunately I fell and damaged my knee, requiring stitches, just before going to the RAF Parachute Training School at Abingdon. This did not make things easier there but I just managed to escape the wrath of the Parachute Jumping Instructor (PJI). I was about twenty years older than most of my fellow students on the course, which meant that I had to lead from the front and pretend that I liked using the 'fan' and other fiendish parachute training devices.

People ask if one is frightened of jumping out of aeroplanes. On the whole if you are not at all apprehensive your name should be 'Harpic', *ie* clean round the bend. For me it was a case of being afraid of being afraid. As I sat in an aeroplane waiting to jump out I was not so much afraid of the actual exit through the open door as of doing something silly on the way down and hitting the ground too hard. At 39 years of age, having had a disc removed from my spine, this was my not unreasonable fear, while the average young soldier sitting along with me was probably afraid of the actual exit, though he might not admit it.

I was much heartened during this para training and on other similar occasions by the presence with me of Leslie Leadbitter, my batman. He had been with me in the jungle in Malaya and on exercises in Germany and voluntarily came on with me to this parachuting world. He was a heavy chap and I know he disliked parachuting but he stuck it out. He was loyal and stout-hearted and a great companion.

After an intensive period of ground training at Abingdon we were pronounced fit for jumping at Weston-on-the-Green, the other side of Oxford. In order to take advantage of the supposedly light winds in the early morning we were involved in a number of tense, nervy dawn starts followed by postponements and cancellations. At last a suitable day dawned and we carried out our first two jumps from a balloon before breakfast.

Initial jumps are made from a balloon because there is no slipstream. At first going up in the cage underneath the balloon is quite fun and there is some ribaldry among the five occupants. Suddenly all is quiet except for the swoosh of the balloon above. People on the ground become very small and one is confronted by the monstrous folly of what one has let oneself in for. The balloon comes to a juddering halt and the cage tilts forward to the bar at the entrance which is opened leaving a very empty space. A blue flag is waved on the ground, the PJI shouts 'Go' and, startled, one is out, whether of one's own volition or a push one will never know. There is a sensation of falling and one sees one's boots above (heavier than the head). Horrors, it's not going to open. Suddenly a series of little clicks, a whoosh and there it is, that wonderful sight of an open canopy above. One is now going down the right way up and the PJI on the ground is shouting instructions as how to land. But one is too excited to take any notice and lands in a heap; no marks but too exhilarated to care.

Quite soon a second jump from the balloon takes place. This, if anything, is more unpleasant than the first as there is no longer a sense of braving the unknown. But it is tackled, a better landing made and an unforgettable dawn is over.

Next came jumps from aircraft and the problems that can arise when getting out into the slipstream which can cause the rigging lines of the chute to be twisted on opening. The correct action to unravel them must be taken quickly.

One early morning I made a bad landing and hit my tail hard. It was so sore that when we got back to Abingdon I took it to the experienced RAF doctor. He took one look at the scar on my bared backside and said: 'You've had a laminectomy, you should never jump.' Although inwardly I might have agreed with him I replied that I had entered this operation on my joining form, had made no attempt to hide it, was passed fully fit, had already jumped and proposed to continue to do so. 'Well,' he said, 'I'm afraid I shall have to report it.' He then examined the damage, which was a badly bruised cocyx which remains sore to this day.

Feeling rather low I went out of the Medical Centre to be confronted by an excited PJI who said: 'Oh sir, I've been looking for you everywhere. The weather has improved and we have got an aircraft. We're emplaning straight away.'

I got into the Hastings with a backside too sore to sit on the hard tin seats, having been medically advised that I should never jump. It was a calm autumn afternoon and I floated down quietly and made a stand-up landing to save my bottom. This was only allowed to be done by experts and was almost a court martial offence. When I explained the circumstances I was forgiven.

The OC of the PTS, Wing-Commander Jimmy Blythe, was very considerate and allowed me to complete the course including the night descent and so earn my wings. But now I endured a prolonged medical battle.

A medical staff officer at Aldershot, on receiving the report from the doctor at Abingdon, took it upon himself to decree that I could not command a parachute battalion and informed everyone accordingly. Maybe I should not have parachuted, but the Army had invited me to do so in full knowledge of my medical history. I was now a qualified parachutist and was determined to continue. But I had to fight it all the way.

I demanded and got a War Office Medical Board. I got the distinguished surgeon who had operated on my back, Mr R.H. Young, to give evidence. He said that a laminectomy made no difference to one's capability to parachute: in his view if one was foolish enough to want to do it one was just as likely to break one's neck as back or anything else. The Board passed me A1 fit for everything with no restrictions.

Armed with this I badgered the Military Secretary who re-appointed me to command 3 Para six weeks late. That Medical staff officer (an Australian surgeon) cost me some seniority and much anguish. Not a good way for a newcomer to enter the Maroon Machine.

Mike Walsh had successfully completed the parachute course following mine and so we found ourselves arriving together at Corunna Barracks. Incidentally I was to spend an inordinate amount of my time trying to persuade people to make the Barracks fit for the Army's best soldiers to live in. It was a Herculean task. Aldershot has subsequently been rebuilt but at that time the 100-year-old accommodation made a terrible 'home' for soldiers and families alike.

We had arrived not long before Christmas: a time for parties. It was customary for soldiers who had completed their three years' voluntary service as a parachutist to hold a demob party. Obviously these were lively affairs. During one of these soon after our arrival the participants fell foul of the Royal Naval Police in Portsmouth and rather roughly saw them off. At least it did not take place on our own doorstep but it caused a stir in Aldershot; so much so that the District Commander felt he could not attend our Officers' Christmas Ball. An odd decision, but we did not let it spoil the party.

Early in the New Year another group had a row with the Civil Police in Aldershot on a Friday night and assaulted one of them. The Police insisted on finding all the culprits and the investigations took time. I decided to make up the lost training time by carrying it out over the weekend. I also suspended leave passes and decreed that all ranks, including married officers and men, should remain in barracks for that weekend. It was really little different from an exercise in the field. However, a mole leaked this to the *Sunday Pictorial* who late on Saturday night tackled me on the phone about 'mass punishment'.

Direct dealings with the Press by lowly lieutenant-colonels were far from encouraged in those days but I had to say something and gave an explanation authorised by the Brigade Commander. Needless to say, little of it appeared in that paper on Sunday and the entire Press corps descended on me. Most of them accepted my explanation with the exception of the *Daily Mirror*. The Police completed their investigations during the day and I was able to relax the restrictions by the evening.

When I addressed the Battalion the next day I referred to the headline in the *Sunday Pictorial* – '200 Army Wives Sleep Alone' – and said: 'Well, we hope they did.' This relaxed any tension and the whole business brought us all together so that some good came out of the unfortunate affair. It became a 3 Para joke for many years to come.

But there was to be one more such incident. Later in the year, just before we went to the Brigade Camp at Stanford Training Area in Suffolk, some hot heads considered that the Sappers in the neighbouring barracks had become too tiresome and took it upon themselves to teach them a lesson. Perhaps they overdid it and it became a little rough. Anyway it was ill-received at District Headquarters; another 3 Para 'incident' and, as the person in command, I was told they must stop or I might not be considered fit to remain in charge. Very unfair but there it was.

When we all arrived in camp I took my life and career in my hands and got up in front of the Battalion and told them all this. I ended up by saying: 'If you want to get rid of me as your CO just go and do this sort of thing again.' They never did.

But don't get me wrong. We were a highly professional airborne unit who played hard and worked harder.

There was plenty of sport for which many had joined the Army. Competition between units in the Parachute Brigade was intense. Appropriately, cricket and hockey were our best sports. I captained the Aldershot District cricket side which had a very good fixture list and played on the excellent Club ground. I made some good scores for them but was not so successful for the Battalion though we managed to win the Brigade competition. We had a superb hockey side and had high hopes of winning the Army Championship.

Most important, training: the Parachute soldier wants to be a fit, fighting man, master of his weapons, and applies himself to his individual training. Next comes the forming of trained teams. I set an exercise for each platoon which involved parachuting on to Bodmin Moor in Cornwall, navigating through the bogs at night and ending up with a dawn attack on Trevose Head golf course. Not a bad place to see at dawn if one must.

Time only allowed me to jump with one platoon but I jumped with each of the company exercises. I also jumped on three battalion exercises, all without trouble and so the doubts about my parascending were dissolved.

In the spring we were honoured by a visit from His Royal Highness the Duke of Edinburgh. The Colonel Commandant of the Parachute Regiment, Field-Marshal Montgomery of Alamein was present and all units of the Brigade Group took part. The three Battalions of the Parachute Regiment paraded with Colours and Mascots. We were particularly proud of our Mascot, a lovely grey Welsh pony called Samswn and presented by Vivian Street.

The Infantry marched past, followed by a drive past by the transport of all units. Some of these such as the Sappers and Workshops included some large, heavy vehicles. HRH expressed surprise at the amount of this type of transport, doubting whether it could take part in an airborne assault. In this he was quite right and subsequently changes were made and the technique of the heavy drop developed.

In the summer I was delighted to welcome Geoffrey Howlett who had made a big effort to join me from our parent Regiment. He was followed by several other good officers. The Colonel of the Queen's Own, General Oliver, was very broadminded and encouraged officers to do a tour in my Battalion. The newly created Parachute Regiment at first consisted only of other ranks, the officers being seconded for short tours. This led to an anomalous situation. A lively, active creation consisted of a body – the soldiers; a heart – the sergeants' mess; but there was no head, a necessity however wooden. It was soon to be rectified.

The Brigade Commander, Desmond Gordon, was off sick for a time during which I was in acting command of the Brigade. An additional burden for a newcomer to the airborne world who was struggling to perfect his own unit. However, we coped thanks to the support of a very competent brigade staff.

And so a very busy and hectic year went by. Christmas came and we had ourselves another Ball. We did not invite the District Commander.

By now we were in pretty good order ready for anything including the unexpected, which was about to hit us.

16
Cyprus

Utrinque Paratus – Motto of The Parachute Regiment

All of the Battalion were still away on Christmas block leave when the Brigade Major phoned me and said, 'Colonel, there's trouble in Jordan. British residents are at risk. Your Battalion has to fly out to Cyprus ready to help them.' 'OK,' I said, 'When?' 'Thursday', he replied. It was then Monday so there was a great deal to be done in a very short time. But it was done and away we went. That's what a parachute battalion is all about.

We emplaned at Blackbushe airfield just off the A30 which was convenient. But we travelled in Shackletons, a slow long-range aircraft operated by RAF Coastal Command and in no way designed for troop-carrying. On landing for fuel in Malta my plane damaged its undercarriage. Not wishing to be delayed, I hastily left my seat with the crew, dashed up the runway and scrambled into the back of the plane in front just before it took off. I thus added myself to an already crowded compartment from which there was no escape and it was very uncomfortable indeed. It seemed a very long way from Malta to Cyprus in the back of a Shackleton.

However, on arrival at Nicosia in the middle of the night there was the pleasure of being met by my old boss, Sir Charles Keightley, now C-in-C Middle East Land Forces (MELF).

MELF had left Egypt the previous year, some to Libya and others to Cyprus which was ill-equipped to cope with them. There was virtually no permanent accommodation. The Keightleys lived 'in luxury' in what had been a quartermaster's house – a far cry from Flagstaff House, Singapore. They were very kind to me, often asking me to meals and allowing me the use of their bathroom, a great treat.

1 Para arrived a day after us and as we were officially 'in transit' we were accommodated in a tented transit camp hastily erected on what had been a football ground. Cyprus in January can be quite wet and it certainly was this year; also the nights were jolly cold. Mud was a great trial.

We settled in with the minimum of kit and trained to get acclimatised and ready for the next bit of action. After a month of stand-by during confused events in Jordan, Glub Pasha was invited to depart by King Hussein and things settled down there. So we were not needed.

But could we rejoice and go home? Not likely!

We had been drawn into the Cyprus scene and to play a part in the struggle against the Greek terrorist organisation known as EOKA. The internal security situation in the island was grave. Briefly, some Greek-Cypriots wanted ENOSIS, union with Greece. The extremists formed this terrorist organisation which was ably led by a Greek Army Colonel, George Grivas. He was an evil nuisance, but one had to admire him as an outstanding guerilla leader. EOKA were a nasty lot who committed murders and atrocities against their own people as well as ourselves. It was unlike Malaya where we went into the jungle knowing that while the terrorists might attack and kill us, the women and children were quite safe in the cities. In Cyprus while we were out chasing terrorists in the mountains, Service wives were being murdered in Nicosia.

We did not hide behind batons and shields but stood for no nonsense when confronted by stone-throwing youths and the like. We fixed bayonets and marched calmly towards the crowd which rapidly melted away. The buzz got around and we were rarely attacked.

Operating under semi-active service conditions, we were liable to suffer more casualties a result of accidents than action by EOKA. We always went out armed with one up the spout. However strict the rules about clearing the weapon accidents will happen. Driving was often hazardous too. As a reminder of the dangers at one time a notice appeared at the entrance to Tunisia Camp bearing a skull and crossbones and the following:

Ashes to ashes
Dust to dust
If EOKA don't get you
3 PARA must.

A delicate episode concerned Archbishop Makarios. I was whipped off the hockey field to take a party of men and arrest him in his 'palace' in Nicosia. We took him straight to the airfield and he was flown off to the Seychelles. We then had the unpleasant task of cordoning and searching the palace which was next to a girls' school where the young ladies were most hostile and stoned us. We could not march against them.

Other operations were quite different, especially against gangs in the Troodos mountains. They rise to 6,000ft from the Nicosia plain and are mainly forest-clad; snowbound in winter, delightful in summer. Acting on information we carried out major operations, sometimes in conjunction with the Royal Marines and other units.

One of these was code-named 'Lucky Alphonse'. Lucky it certainly was not. It started promisingly with the discovery of a terrorist hide. Ambushes were laid but an unauthorised patrol from 1 Para strayed across the inter-unit boundary into one of our ambush positions and a Sergeant-Major was shot and killed. At dawn when there was no movement by our troops a person was seen approaching our positions in the forest dressed in a grey garment with no hat. He did not answer a challenge and fitted the bill for a terrorist exactly and he too was shot. But he turned out to be a feverish soldier from another unit who had wandered away during the night wrapped in a blanket and was hopelessly lost.

A patrol of 'C' Company led by Sergeant Scott, moving in very steep, rocky terrain, suddenly sighted a group of men about 100yds away. They dashed at them but during the time it took to cover the difficult ground all the terrorists managed to get away. They fled leaving everything, weapons and kit, including Grivas's diary and photos. There were not enough wireless sets for every patrol and as luck would have it, Sergeant Scott had not got one. So it was some time before news of this action reached me. Efforts were redoubled to catch Grivas but we never did.

But far worse was still to come. A forest fire was started which burned for several days. Suddenly fanned by a wind, the flames burst upon us and roared up through the dry pine forest. It claimed some thirty lives mainly from other units but including Captain Mike Beagley and his driver, Private Hawker, who were only bringing out the mail from camp. Mike Walsh escaped with minor burns by running into and out of the flames instead of trying to run away from them.

We did have some successes, often based on patient and cunning undercover work. A particularly good one was conducted by the Machine-Gun Platoon commander, Mike Newall. A very successful ambush was carried out by Sgt Howse, also from the Machine-Gun Platoon.

Amidst all these goings-on there was plenty of sport and we beat most people at most things, including winning the MELF Hockey Championship after a fierce final against 40 Field Regiment, RA.

Jazz was not neglected either. As well as encouraging the Band to play this kind of music, I used to perform at a joint in Kyrenia called the Harbour Club which was run by Roy and Judy Finlay. Judy had been a well-known singer in the English radio and dance band scene and was a delight to sing with. They always had a top class jazz pianist and I accompanied him both vocally and on a crude form of string bass made literally of string and a soap box.

Our Band under the young, lively Bandmaster Crossman came out in May and lived with us in Tunisia Camp. They were very good value both musically and practically. We put on an excellent Beating of Retreat shortly before we went to Suez. Then as we were preparing to go they helped with the running of the camp, freeing parachutists for action. We would have been hard put to manage without them.

Throughout all this time I had been blessed with having as second-in-command one of the best and nicest officers from the Queen's Own RWK Regiment, Mike Grove, who gave me loyal support and friendship. His tour with the Parachute Regiment ended in mid-summer and he was replaced by the very competent Dennis Beckett from the Essex Regiment.

16 Para Brigade had been split between Nicosia and Aldershot so that the Brigade Commander, the dynamic Tubby Butler, was always dashing between the two places. However, after Nasser had nationalised the Suez Canal the rest of the Brigade Group was sent out to join us.

In August the Battalion was flown home to train with RAF Transport Command for an airborne assault operation. This was marvellous and although there was a great deal to be done in three weeks, including two Battalion drops on Salisbury Plain, I allowed the maximum leave possible. I asked everyone to turn up on time at Blackbushe for the return flight and they all did. This was the first time we had seen our families for eight months: I suspect many a budding para resulted. We also collected our reservists who had been called back to the Colours and took them back with us. Almost without exception they behaved splendidly and were a welcome addition to the Battalion.

Tubby Butler had worked wonders with his American friends and obtained six of their brand new anti-tank guns, the 106mm. We learned to fire them and took them to Cyprus. They were to prove a winner in battle.

We spent September back in Cyprus at its hottest, training and planning for an airborne operation in Egypt. By the beginning of October things seemed to have quietened down and we returned to chasing EOKA. At the end of the month the whole Battalion was deployed in small patrols throughout the Troodos Range when I was told to return to Tunisia Camp as quickly as possible and prepare in earnest for war.

17

Suez: Mounting the Airborne Assault

Trust in God, but keep your powder dry – Oliver Cromwell

It was on a Monday, 29 October, that we trekked back from the cool mountains to our hot, dusty camp next to the airfield where it was apparent that there was a lot of activity and many more planes. I did not then know that on the following Monday one of those planes would deposit me with others on the sands of Egypt.

On that first Monday I was told to prepare for an airborne operation but I was not told where or when.

Now although we were well trained, fighting fit and ready for action there is always a great deal to be done before launching into the airborne version. Items of airborne equipment have to be prised out of Ordnance who do not always appreciate that the lack of a peculiar nail may well cause the loss of a vital piece of equipment if not a life. Parachutes have to be obtained and fitted. What to take with you – bullets, food, water – has to be decided and loaded. Synthetic airborne training needs to be done to refresh everyone on aircraft drills and parachute techniques. Wireless sets and batteries have to be prepared.

All this and more was carried out and successfully completed under the direction and watchful eye of the Second-in-Command, Dennis Beckett, now a brevet lieutenant-colonel. So we now had two colonels, which I trusted would prove to be over-insurance.

Meanwhile I had to make a plan. It helps if you know how many transport planes you have, which I did not. So the plan had to be kept simple and flexible, ready to meet constantly changing circumstances.

It was not until the Thursday that the Brigade Commander, Tubby Butler, was authorised to brief me as to the exact task of the battalion group. Even then the date was still uncertain. Put simply, our task was to capture El Gamil Airfield, Port Said, advance east to the edge of the town and link up with the seaborne Royal Marines: we were also to prevent any reinforcements coming in from the west. To do this my Force consisted of the following:

3 Para, with under command:
Detachment 33 Para Field Regiment, RA
3 Troop 9 Independent Para Field Squadron, RE
Detachment 16 Independent Para Brigade Signal Squadron
Detachment Para Platoon 63 Company, RASC
Detachment 23 Para Field Ambulance RAMC
13 Air Contact Team
Detachment Brigade RAF Para Det.

Tubby Butler added himself and his Brigade Major, Charles Dunbar, as a very small tactical brigade headquarters to co-ordinate the British and French para landings.

Although each seat was very precious I agreed that one should be allocated to a member of the Press on the understanding that he had some knowledge of parachuting. Somehow Peter Wood of the *Daily Mirror* managed to con his colleagues that he was an experienced parachutist and so got the vacancy.

He was a big man and unfortunately not a parachutist at all. In the event he had a heavy landing, damaged his ankles, and evacuated himself on the first available helicopter.

I was upset by all this as I am always in favour of working openly with the Press and felt that a representative accompanying me on that first day could have told the true story of our humane treatment of the Egyptians and dispelled the baseless lies and figments of imagination that were put about afterwards by people who weren't there.

The number of serviceable transport planes changed right up to the last minute. Finally there were 18 Valettas, 7 Hastings (personnel) and 7 Hastings (heavy drop). This allowed us to be dropped as follows:

First lift 'P hour'	Personnel:	668
	Transport:	7 jeeps, 4 trailers, 6 anti-tank guns
	Containers:	176
Second lift 'P+8 hours'	Personnel:	58
	Transport:	3 jeeps, one trailer
	Containers:	36
	Panniers:	48

The containers were carefuly packed with essential engineer, signal and medical stores. Some were bound to get lost or damaged but if all went well we could expect the following maximum scales of major ammunition:

In the first lift:	10,000 rounds per MMG (4 × MMGs)
	120 HE and 16 Smoke per 3″ mortar (4 × 3″ mortars
	16 rounds per anti-tank gun (6 × 106mm)
In the second lift:	6,000 rounds per MMG
	70 HE per 3″ mortar
	16 rounds per anti-tank gun.

Not a lot with which to fight a battle.

The dropping zone (DZ) was to be the airfield itself which was fairly long but narrow, being largely surrounded by water. The planes were to fly in from west to east into the sun. Accurate navigation and despatch timing were vital as there was very little room for mistakes.

I made and stuck to a basic plan which allowed for changes in detail. One Company ('A' Coy) was to jump out first from each plane and secure the dropping zone, the airfield, at the west end.

Another company ('B' Coy) was to jump last and secure the far end of the DZ. These two companies were to carry out these tasks without waiting for further orders.

A third company ('C' Coy) was to drop in the middle and concentrate ready for action as my reserve.

Elements of Support company and Headquarters were fitted in as best they could be.

A fourth company ('D' Coy), organised from those who had to help mount the operation, was to come in on the second lift.

Each parachutist was loaded into the aircraft with this plot in mind, *ie* it was where he was required to hit the ground that was the governing factor, not the order of the fly-in of the planes. Each aircraft had men from different companies in it so that the loss of any particular plane would not prove a disaster. Everyone knew where to go when he landed and what he had to do, and elaborate rallying processes were not needed.

This may sound obvious now but it was a new airborne technique then and required accurate planning and liaison with the Air Planning Staff. This was admirably carried out by the Air Adjutant, Geoffrey Howlett, in close co-operation with the Brigade Air Staff Officer, the brilliant, unflappable Frank King.

In my modest experience the British Army makes admirable plans but is inclined to overlook the fact that the enemy might have something to say about them. The Intelligence world produced virtually no useful information on the exact dispositions of the Egyptian forces confronting me. We might as well have been going to Omsk as Port Said which, considering we had not long left the place and there were British citizens still living there, seems rather extraordinary.

The exception was the air photographs taken by the RAF which were excellent. In fact they were almost too good. As I was dressing in my tent not long before we were due to take off, the Intelligence Officer (IO) Jim Burke, dashed in with the latest ones taken of the DZ, El Gamil Airfield, that day. These showed it to be covered with little black dots which the experts had interpreted as being anti-parachutist explosive devices. It was too late to make any difference so I decided not to lower morale by telling anyone. So only Jim and I enjoyed the flight to Egypt with this uncomfortable thought about our reception on the DZ in the back of our minds.

In the event they turned out to be barrels filled with sand which had been put there to prevent aircraft using the runway. Rather than being hostile they provided comfortable cover against enemy fire on landing.

After the battle we estimated that we had engaged an Egyptian battalion group in our area sited to oppose an airborne or seaborne invasion. One company was located to defend the airfield with two pill-boxes armed with MMGs able to sweep the DZ and manned slit trenches around it. Towards the town a strong company position was located in the cemetery. In this area we captured three MMGs, one six-pounder anti-tank gun, four 81mm mortars and a considerable quantity of LMGs and automtic rifles. Further on there was another company and two 3.7 anti-aircraft guns together with three Russian SU 100 self-propelled guns, virtually tanks. The native quarter was held by the National Guard in strength. In the dock area there were rockets sited to bombard both the beaches and the airfield.

Some individual Egyptian soldiers fought with considerable courage in defence but only very few employed aggressive tactics and no counter attacks were mounted. Considering the large stocks of good weapons and ammunition they had available they did not do very well, especially as for the first twenty-four hours they had to deal only with lightly equipped parachutists.

They made full use of buildings, including hospitals, and some armed men were encountered wearing civilian clothes. I mention these points because of subsequent ill-informed criticisms made by people who were not there.

'Musketeer' was a joint Anglo-French operation and we had some French parachutists in the air with us. We made friends with our namesakes 3rd (Etranger) Parachute Battalion. They were Foreign Legion troops and very tough and experienced, having fought in Indo-China. We envied them their equipment which was light and much more suitable for airborne operations than ours. Also they had a more realistic and practical attitude to their transport planes. They treated their Dakotas like unit trucks and lived with them and slept under them where appropriate. They were ordered to jump and secure the southern exits on the routes leading out of Port Said. A stick of parachutists from the Guards Independent Parachute Squadron and a few Sappers jumped with them with the task of preventing the enemy from blowing the bridges. They succeeded in this and did very well. Another French Para Battalion was to jump and capture Port Fuad on the opposite side of the Canal to Port Said. The place was largely inhabited by French people and after a brief, bitter struggle they were able to occupy it.

So much for enemy, about whom we knew so little, and own troops. On Saturday, 3 November, I got my final orders and in the afternoon briefed all ranks in two sessions on the football field. The camp was sealed and we got ready for the start.

And the start was put forward.

At this time the plan was for the battalion group to drop on Tuesday in conjunction with a bombardment and seaborne assault. But on the Sunday morning I was told that we were to drop on Monday, twenty-four hours ahead of the seaborne assault. Although this obviously increased the hazards considerably, all ranks received the news with pride and gratification. For have no doubts about it the 'Toms' wanted to go and have a crack at Nasser. They were not interested in, and took no notice of, the rantings of some politicans and others at home. They preferred listening to the 'Goon Show' to 'Yesterday in Parliament'. Not that there was much difference.

We had our final briefings during the Sunday morning and in the afternoon carried out a rehearsal of our emplaning on the airfield, including fitting 'chutes. This rehearsal, insisted on by Dennis Beckett, proved invaluable and meant that we were able to get into our planes in good order during the dark the next morning. The actual business of climbing into the plane was quite a performance. Because we were going to be entirely on our own we had to rely on what we could take with us. Weapons containers which are clipped on to the parachutist and released in the air during descent were filled to absolute capacity. All were extremly heavy and those containing parts of mortars and wireless sets even more so. Some soldiers could barely lift their loads. To save weight I took the decision to discard the reserve 'chute which we normally wore. No harm came of this. Horace McClelland, our splendid padre, held a drumhead service for all ranks and we were ready to go.

I myself was able to slip out and take a quick cup of tea with the Allied Commander-in-Chief, General Sir Charles Keightley, and Lady Keightley at their house. He was concerned to explain to me why he had had to send us off on our own before the arrival of the main seaborne force. Basically it was because the Israelis were going so fast that someone had to get to the Canal before they reached it.

So much for collusion.

18

Suez: The Airborne Assault

Theirs not to reason why – Tennyson

True to form, 'Operation Musketeer' began at dawn at our end when the first transport aircraft taxied off from Nicosia at 0415hrs for the three-hour flight to Port Said where 'P' hour was at 0715 GMT.

(We worked on GMT although time in the Middle East is two hours ahead, so dawn for us was around 4am and it started to get dark about 3.30pm.)

For us the flight was uneventful. Most of the soldiers managed to doze but I had too much on my mind and tried to read. As we approached the Egyptian coast I was heartened to see below us three destroyers thinking they might arrive to support us in the battle later. But this was not to be as they were still some twenty-four hours' steaming away. Happily the aircraft carriers were there, as we shall see.

For the RAF some difficulties were caused by an unexpected headwind which slowed down the heavily laden Hastings. I was in one of the leading Valettas of 114 Squadron which dropped us precisely on time. As I stood in the door during the run-in I could see a smoke marker which had been dropped by a Canberra and then the airfield before us, just as in the photos. A building by the control tower was burning, having been hit by an air strike; the barrels were there too.

And then I was in the air and, *DG*, made a reasonable landing on sand not the concrete runway. As one floated down one was reminded that it was indeed Guy Fawkes Day as there were coloured lights, flashes and explosions everywhere. The difference being that we were on the receiving end of these bangs which, far from being empty, contained lethal bits of metal. It was essential to get cracking quickly which everyone did.

Changes had to be made in the order of fly-in but it did not matter much. Five aircraft had to make double runs to ensure the successful delivery of all their loads. Two trailers candled in, but in spite of the heavy personal loads there was only one parachuting injury, a great tribute to all concerned. In ten minutes the majority of the force were on the ground in the right place, a magnificent effort by the RAF. There was some flak and five Hastings and two Valettas were found to have been hit but none was shot down.

There were the usual crop of hairy parachuting stories. Particularly affected were members of 'B' Company who had to get out of the plane at the end of the stick quickly before they were deposited in the town of Port Said. This nearly happened to Private Peter Lamph who fell as he was crossing the spar and eventually jumped so late that the plane was homeward bound. He came down in the sea and immediately came under fire. He feigned dead in the water for some time and as the attack by his comapny progressed was able to scramble up the beach and eventually join up with them. Some time later Group-Captain Brian

McNamara sent him a crate of beer with the compliments of RAF Transport Command to compensate him for his wetting. Another member of 'B' Company, Private Looker, landed right on the enemy defences at the end of the airfield. As he descended he saw an Egyptian had climbed out of his slit trench in order to get a better shot at him. He managed to manoeuvre his heavy weapons container swinging below him so that it knocked the Egyptian back into his slit trench. This was too much for the Egyptian and Looker was able to overpower him immediately on landing. This was just as well as it took all of thirty seconds to get a weapon out of one's container.

Private Neal, a medic, also had trouble with the spar in the Valetta and jumped late, landing in the sewage farm. He had to crawl back from enemy lines under fire from both sides but managed to get through safely bringing with him his valuable load of surgical equipment.

I have indicated that we arrived to quite a warm reception with a variety of hostile stuff being deposited on the dropping zone (DZ) from all directions. The immediate necessity was to clear the enemy positions on and around the airfield.

At the west end Major Mike Walsh's 'A' Company went into swift action. A patrol under Sergeant Legg occupied the blazing control buildings and tower. The first person to arrive at the tower was Private Frank Eccles who, having just missed the roof, got tangled up in a palm tree at the entrance. He dangled there until released by his amused mates.

Fire was coming from a machine-gun post at the west end and Mike watched whilst a platoon under 2nd-Lieutenant Peter Coates carried out a copy book action to knock it out. During this, Private Clements distinguished himself by scoring a direct hit on the pill box with the rocket launcher.

At the other end towards the town 'B' Company were getting on with things equally vigorously but not without struggles and casualties as the opposition was stronger. The Company Commander, Major Dick Stevens, led a charge against the enemy and was hit in the hand but carried on after having an injection of morphia from his second-in-command, Karl Beale.

Meanwhile I collected my command team which consisted of Leslie Leadbitter, my batman; Ray Issitt of the Army Physical Training Corps, my bodyguard; my signaller, and Major Geoff Norton, OC Support Company. We went off to the front to see what was happening to 'B' Company.

My role was to support company commanders where I could without interfering. My other important task was to try to deal with enemy positions firing at us from a distance. This I did through the weapons of Support Company and by air strikes by the Fleet Air Arm. They were controlled through a parachuted Air Contact Team consisting of Major Tony Stephens, Captain Bill Hancock and the French Liaison Officer, François Collet, a splendid character. They did an excellent job and the close air support was superb. I soon came to have complete confidence in the accuracy of the pilots and called for strikes as near as 400yds to our own troops. They were a battle-winning factor and at the end of the day I sent the following signal to the Royal Navy:

'Many thanks for your magnificent support to us this day which thrilled all ranks. Its timely effectiveness and accuracy were beyond praise and undoubtedly saved us many casualties. Please convey our gratitude to all ranks.'

The Mortar Platoon had its problems as one mortar was damaged in the drop and only three were in use until after the resupply. The platoon commander, Captain Norman Morley, was hit by a splinter of shrapnel on his helmet. He remained but was *hors de combat* for a while. The platoon was most ably handled by Sergeant Wright who combined the roles of mobile fire controller and commander.

Tubby Butler joined me but at no time interfered and just gave me his inspiring support. The 'Toms' were glad to see him.

I took stock and found that in half-an-hour we had cleared and secured the airfield. In spite of considerable enemy fire our casualties had so far been comparatively light. I appreciated that we must now advance and carry out the task of clearing the enemy defences as far as the native quarter, as ordered.

The terrain over which we had to operate was a curious mixture. It varied from flat sand and sand dunes (the dropping zone) through very thick reeds, marshes and ditches (the sewage farm), across a large cemetery containing graves and stone memorials of all denominations on into a wooden shanty town and, finally, a built up area. There was water on both sides making a small frontage and allowing virtually no room for deployment or encirclement.

Dick Stevens set about clearing the sewage farm. First 5 Platoon under Sergeant 'Pompey' Norman on the left cleared about halfway through the farm. 4 Platoon under 2nd-Lieutenant Chris Hogg pushed through thick reeds containing snipers and occupied the buildings at the righthand edge of the farm. Pushing on, their reward was to be strafed by two French Myster fighters and they had to fling themselves into the foul sewage. At least this ensured that no one was hurt. François took urgent action with the French to ensure that it did not happen again. Their excuse was that they could not believe that we had got so far in so short a time and mistook us for Egyptians. Chris Hogg, now head of Courtaulds, was not amused.

I brought up a machine-gun section which gave good covering fire, also one of the new anti-tank guns. Under the direction of Lieutenant Bill Hill this gun knocked out what we believed to be a dug-in tank on the beach by the cemetery. They also put a round through a house being used as an observation post.

On reaching the end of the sewage farm, 'B' Company came under fire from the cemetery which was a strong position. As I was talking to Dick Stevens about our next move there came a burst of fire which hit him in the leg and he had to be evacuated. So Karl Beale took over.

'B' Company had done enough and it was time to employ a fresh company. I decided to make a full scale attack on the cemetery with as much covering fire as I could muster. The quiet, experienced Major Ron Norman brought up his 'C' Company through mortar fire for the attack.

'H' hour was 1030hrs. The attack was preceded by an airstrike at precisely 1028hrs on the cemetery 400yds away. It was very accurate and the Venoms and Sea Hawks of the Fleet Air Arm succeeded in breaching the strong wall surrounding the cemetery. 7 and 9 Platoons advanced across the sand dunes two minutes later supported by mortar fire for three minutes and by the MMGs. Sgt Howse found an excellent forward position for his section in the sewage buildings with 4 Platoon. From there Geoff Norton and I were able to watch the progress of the attack.

Another text-book attack was most successful and, fighting through to the far end of the cemetery, 'C' Company were able to call for air strikes on a large block of flats facing them which were being used as observation posts by the Eygptians. Ron sent patrols forward to them and the Coastguard barracks and dominated the area.

They captured a lot of enemy weapons including three Russian self-propelled guns. Fortunately for Private David Beech, one of these weapons failed to work at a vital moment. Advancing through the graves he heard a noise behind him and, swinging round, found himself confronted by an Egyptian with a rocket launcher. But the mechanism failed and he was able to despatch his enemy with a short burst from his Bren gun. This was typical of the muddled and dangerous fighting in the cemetery.

On the other flank Lieutenant Mike Newall, MMG Platoon commander, advanced down the coast road and captured a Bren-Gun Carrier assisted by Sergeant Davidson of 'C' Company. They quickly got it going and then used it to silence an enemy machine-gun post in the flats. Good, courageous stuff but unorthodox to say the least and it very nearly ended in tragedy. As Mike drove back in triumph to our lines he was spotted by the Number One gunner of one of our anti-tank guns. He promptly fired two spotter rounds, the second making a direct hit. He was about to fire a shell to destroy the carrier when Sergeant Howse rushed up shouting 'Don't shoot, don't shoot! That's Mr Newall'.

So the carrier and its foolhardy driver survived to join our mixed bag of 'liberated' transport on the airfield. The first of this was an old truck which the medical sergeant, 'Jersey' Rabet, had found in the airport garage. It had flat tyres but he managed to make good use of it as an ambulance.

A great deal of life-saving medical work was being done in this garage which Major Norman Kirby of the Para Field Ambulance converted into a Dressing Station and performed vital emergency operations. During one of these the Adjutant, Gerald Mullins, walked in and very quickly hurried out. But he went away to ask the Royal Navy to help us evacuate the most urgent cases.

Half-an-hour later a Naval helicopter landed in a cloud of dust by the control tower. Anxious not to lose his machine by enemy action he kept his rotors running. With some difficulty two stretcher and three sitting cases were loaded and he was off. A gratefully received help, but the number of urgent cases was growing.

Circling overhead was a Dakota which the French used as an aerial command post. The Sappers had removed the drums from the runway and they could see it was clear. So, regardless of the occasional stonks still arriving on the airfield, Colonel De Fouquières decided to land. The Dakota swept down the runway and taxied over to the control buildings. They said they could take eight cases back to Nicosia.

During his descent our charming unit Medical Officer, Sandy Cavenagh, felt something hit him in the eye. He carried on for five hours though it was serious. He was loath to evacuate himself but the sensible Norman Kirby solved the situation by telling him to look after the seriously wounded, especially a man who needed a drip plasma to be kept going properly. So the reluctant Sandy was back in Nicosia less than twelve hours since he had left it. Fortunately his eye responded to treatment and he rejoined us when we returned. We have always been very grateful to Colonel de Fouquières for landing his plane so early in the proceedings long before anyone else.

Later, further helicopter flights were made from the Carriers *HMS Bulwark* and *HMS Albion*, taking away the rest of the wounded and bringing with them supplies of drinks and cigarettes – gifts from the ships' companies for which we were most grateful.

People on the DZ had been busy carrying out the important task of uncrating the vehicles and collecting the stores and ammunition which was running short and I continually had to check it. We lost over seventy 3″ mortar bombs in the drop and only fifteen rounds per mortar could be alloted for 'C' Company's attack, leaving fifteen for further developments. This work was ably organised by Geoff Norton and Regimental Quarter Master Sergeant 'Chippy' Robinson, a real airborne veteran.

At 1315hrs, bang on time, five Hastings and two Valettas appeared in the sky bringing welcome reinforcements. The leading Hastings contained passengers, soldiers who had done a stirling job in launching us in good order and were now panting to get into the action. This they did, arriving by parachute accurately on El Gamil airfield, all fifty-eight of them.

All except one.

Corporal Brackpool of the Paymaster's staff was standing in the door of a Valetta when suddenly the plane banked steeply about a mile west of the DZ. Caught off balance with his heavy weapons container, he fell out. He landed in the sea the wrong side of the river and the destroyed bridge. He had to strip down to his underpants to get across and reached the sand dunes defenceless. Inevitably a number of the natives appeared out of nowhere and were to be seen approaching. Normally one could be expected to be offered eggs or a sister. But this time their intentions seemed more hostile than normal. Happily a patrol under the admirable Officers' Mess Sergeant had been sent out to rescue Brackpool and, like the cavalry, arrived in the nick of time. On their way Sergeant Vokes and his men came under fire from a pillbox in the dunes which had somehow escaped attention earlier. They dealt with this, smartly killing two and taking a number of prisoners with no loss to themselves. All this was done by the so-called 'employed' men of the battalion.

The reception of the drop had been efficiently organised by our RAF Parachute Officer, the imperturbable Flight-Lieutenant Stan Roe, assisted by Parachute Jumping Instructor Sergeant Birchley. They had all the necessary flares and things to satisfy the navigators. The pilots must have found the fly-in more agreeable than their previous one as there was now no flak, the AA fire having been disposed of by us.

To return to the main front which was now with 'C' Company on the town side of the cemetery, where I was standing with Ron Norman. Getting through the cemetery had not been without incident for my command team. As I clambered across the graves an Egyptian soldier popped up from behind a headstone pointing a weapon at me. Before he could use it my bodyguard very promptly disposed of him with his Sten gun. Ray Issitt, our Physical Training Instructor, was not only a brilliant games player, having represented Great Britain at hockey, but was also the Brigade champion Sten-gun shot, very quick on the draw; the right man indeed for a bodyguard!

The important decision of the day had now to be made: to go on or not to go on.

The soldiers were in great heart and raring to go. With the arrival of reinforcements I now had a fourth company who could guard the airfield; also more ammunition. Going flat out along the main axis, I believe we could have reached the docks. However, there were several factors militating against this.

First, it was about to get dark and even the best troops might get mislaid in the mass of byways and alleys of the port at night.

Next, it was not our job. The port was to taken by the seaborne force landing the next day. We had in fact more than carried out our orders and had advanced into the area which was to be bombarded the following morning. Possibly this could be stopped but it was by no means certain and it would be a tragedy if, after having survived a great deal of enemy fire pretty well, we should suffer casualties from our own.

Finally, a main influence on the decision was talk of surrender.

At the same time as our second lift the French dropped another Para battalion in Port Fuad. Their landing was most successful and they gained complete control of the place. Through their contacts it was learned that the Military Commander of Port Said wished to surrender.

After consulting with Tubby Butler it was decided to halt the advance and to remain firm in the sewage farm area for the night. This involved bringing back 'C' Company from the flats and Coastguard Barracks to avoid being in the bombardment area in the morning. It was by no means a withdrawal under enemy pressure, as has been inaccurately implied in some accounts. I repeat that we could have gone on and seized the docks had we been allowed to.

At last light (1530hrs) I had deployed the group as follows:

'B' Company holding the right end of the sewage farm.
'C' Company holding the left end of the sewage farm.
'D' Company holding the west end of the airfield.
'A' Company holding the east end of the airfield.
3 Troop, 9 Para Field Squadron on the airfield.

Meanwhile Tubby Butler and Charles Dunbar had gone off in a helicopter to the French area to draw up the terms of a surrender. During the negotiations we observed a 'Cease Fire' for over two hours.

The Egyptian military commander had been properly brought up, having just returned from an artillery course in Britain at Larkhill and knew when he had done enough and that further unnecessary loss of lives was useless. But he managed to get through to Cairo and was told that on no account was he to surrender and that he could expect help in the morning both from Egyptian troops and from Russia.

Certainly the activities of the Russian Consul in Port Said, Anatoli Tchikov, gave some substance to this. He went round the city distributing weapons to all and sundry, especially the young. He sent loud speaker vans touring the streets shouting 'Fight on people of Port Said! Russian help is coming! Tonight London and Paris will be destroyed by atomic rockets!'

It may sound far fetched now but then, along with the weapons, it was enough to convince the waverers. From the Russian point of view he did a magnificent job; from the Egyptian he cost many, many lives.

Thus sadly the negotiations broke down and firing was resumed. For our part it was very slight and purely defensive. The Egyptians directed some at us but it was mainly amongst themselves. Firing could be heard all night in the city where the newly obtained Russian weapons were being enjoyed and old scores paid off.

My driver, Lance-Corporal Norman Bishop, had uncrated my jeep and we drove back in style along the two miles we had won on foot to main Battalion Headquarters in the airfield buildings where much good work had been going on implementing my instructions and keeping the score. There was little left for me to do and I allowed myself to be persuaded to get some rest. Cosseted by my batman Leslie Leadbitter, I managed to get quite a good night's sleep.

But not everyone was so fortunate especially those in the vicinity of the sewage farm. Apart from the normal precautions against an enemy military attack there were the enemy natural creatures to be reckoned with, especially mosquitoes. It was exceptionally beastly for Chris Hogg and 4 Platoon who, having sampled the safety of the sewage, were particulary tasty targets. They were attacked by myriads of creatures all night and, although tired, could hardly get a wink of sleep. Others of us fared better.

Meanwhile the shooting and killing went on in Port Said.

19
Suez: The Assault from the Sea

War is a pretty rough and dirty game. But politics! –
Field-Marshal The Viscount Montgomery of Alamein

The next morning started with a bang when at dawn a Russian MIG fighter with Egyptian markings carried out a low-level attack on the airfield. This was repeated later in the morning when one soldier was wounded. Afterwards Intelligence staff at Headquarters flatly denied that there had been any attacks by enemy aircraft that day. However, I have plenty of witnesses to confirm that they were wrong.

We drove along the coast road on a beautiful morning to watch the amphibious assault force approach the beaches of Port Said. As the Assault Landing Craft ran into the shore we gave covering fire with MMGs along the beach. It was fascinating to watch an amphibious landing from the enemy's point of view. The previous day we had cleared many of the Egyptian beach defences and had been able to direct airstrikes onto others including gun positions. But for this it is probable that the amphibious forces would have suffered considerably more casualties. Certainly a ship-to-shore milk run could not have been operated in safety by the helicopters in the way it was.

While this was going on 'C' Company sent forward a fighting patrol to reoccupy the cemetery which they did without opposition. Ron Norman then mounted a two-platoon attack across the sand on the Coast Guard Barracks and the flats which were still occupied by snipers. These were captured without loss and a patrol pushed forward to seal off the native quarter.

My Battalion Group had therefore fulfilled the orders given to us and by 0800hrs I was able to report 'Mission Completed. What next?'

I told Mike Walsh to be ready to advance south down the Canal with his 'A' Company Group at the drop of a hat if required.

The Royal Marines were supposed to link up with us but it became apparent that after a comparatively easy landing on the beaches they were having trouble in the town. We could not hang about so I decided to push on into the Marines' area to hasten the link up.

Throughout the morning, despite reports of a 'Cease Fire', enemy mortaring and shelling continued and it was clear that the Egyptians were prepared to fight hard opposite us in the native quarter.

The coast road now forked into two at the outskirts of Port Said. On the left the road continued alongside the beach, and on the right side it went into the native quarter, or 'shanty town', near which were Police Barracks. At the junction of the fork were hospital buildings. The main one was entered without trouble, the staff having fled; but the other, an ophthalmic hospital, was used by the Egyptians as a strongpoint.

A fighting patrol led by Jack Richardson was sent forward to try to meet up with the Marines but were soon met with considerable fire and were pinned down at a building. First Jack's escort, Private Penning, was hit twice in the hand by machine-gun bullets. Then a rocket-launcher bomb hit Jack's rifle; it failed to explode but it carried away the rifle together with the tips of three fingers. At the same time Corporal Stead was hit in the arm by a bullet which shattered his elbow.

Ron Norman had been anxiously following the progress of his patrol from observation posts under fire. He was considering how best to extricate them when it was taken care of in a very unexpected way.

Back at the Dressing Station Captain Malcolm Elliott, the Para Field Ambulance anaesthetist, had been relieved by a keen Naval anaesthetist who had come by helicopter to help. Norman Kirby was continuing to perform operations and more medical supplies were urgently needed. On learning from the Adjutant that a hospital had apparently been captured intact he immediately thought that this was the place to find more medical stores.

Borrowing Gerald's jeep and driver they drove merrily up the road to the main hospital. They had just about reached it when they were fired on by a machine gun in the other hospital building fifty yards away. They managed to turn round and dash back to shelter unscathed.

Malcolm was furious at being fired on from a hospital and when he learned that there were wounded soldiers in the vicinity decided he must do something about it. So driving himself this time he drove under fire to where they were pinned down. He tended their wounds and loaded them into the jeep. He then discovered that he did not know how to engage the reverse gear on a jeep. Every gear he tried only took him a bound out of cover nearer to the enemy.

Sergeant 'Lofty' Read was the only man left unwounded. He undertook to give covering fire with his Bren gun while Malcolm drove towards the enemy and swung round as fast as he could. In spite of the enemy fire he managed to get them all back to safety. He then volunteered to go back to rescue Sergeant Read. But he was told that the sergeant had definitely been killed, and it was not worth the risk to collect a dead body.

The enemy in shanty town and the Police barracks were still resisting actively and causing casualties. So I called for an airstrike on their positions as I had done the previous day. But already political factors were beginning to play their part.

I was told that the airstrike had not been authorised 'to avoid further damage to civilian property'. No matter if casualties were incurred by British soldiers so long as damage was not incurred by Egyptian property. But the message went on to say 'Use own weapons'.

So I did just that with startling results.

I brought up a 106 anti-tank gun which fired five rounds. The results were devastating.

The Police barracks were shattered and the wooden shacks in shanty town caught alight and quickly burned away. In a short time shanty town virtually ceased to exist; probably no bad thing really.

So much for the policy of preserving Egyptian property at a risk to British lives. Possibly the airstrike would have caused much less damage.

Anyway, organised resistance now folded up and the Egyptian soldiers began to melt away. In fact we could see numbers of them putting on their long flowing *ghabadiers* over their uniforms and fleeing south along the Manzala Canal. They

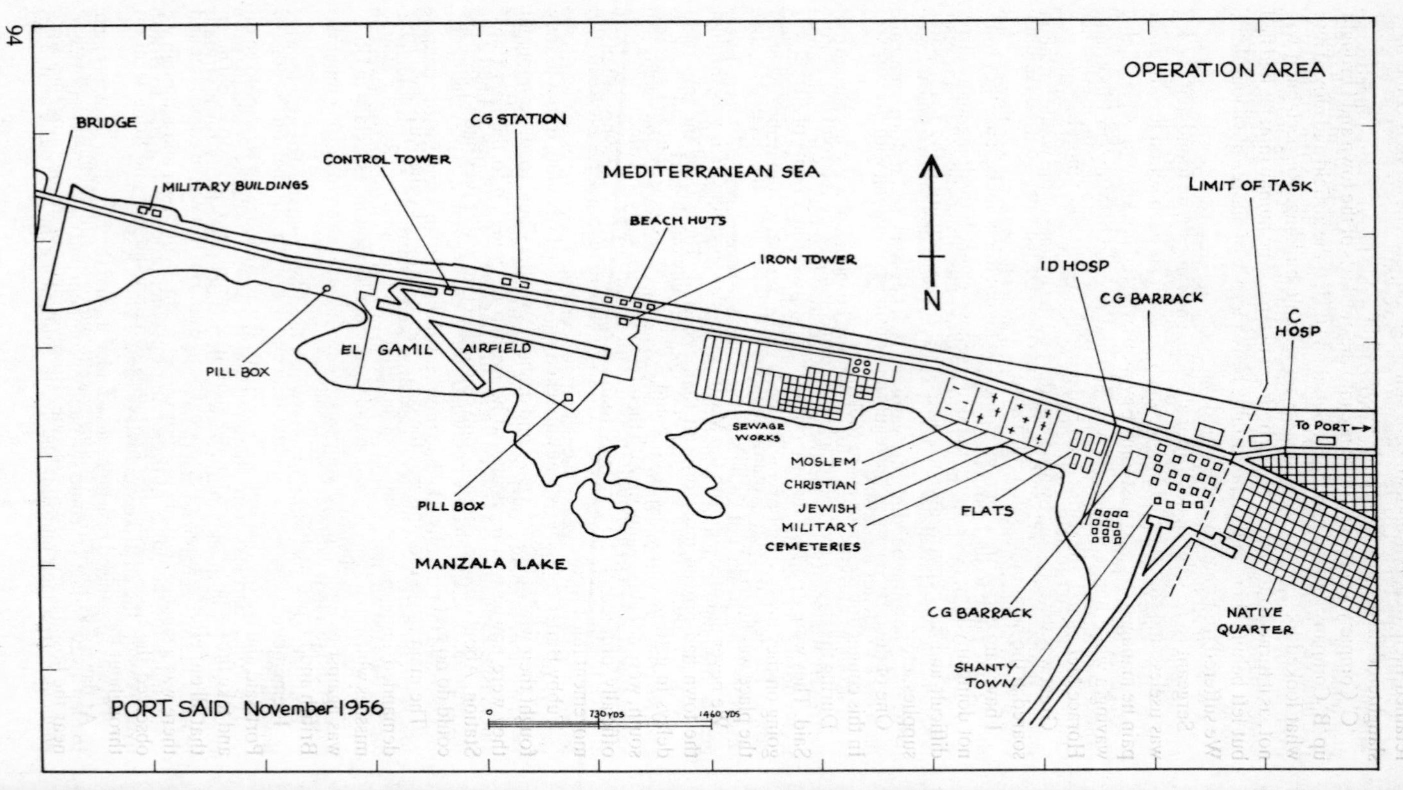

PORT SAID November 1956

retained their weapons and so were still a fair target. The MMGs could have slaughtered them but I forbade them to open fire.

'C' Company were able to advance into the outskirts of the town and I brought up 'B' Company into the flats. Main Battalion HQ left the airfield and moved into what looked like, in the dark, a large respectable building. Respectable it was not, as it turned out to have been a house of ill fame. The human inmates had fled but left behind them in the comfortable beds a legacy of masses of vicious fleas. We suffered from their attention for days.

Sergeant Read was not dead after all. When he came to, he found that one leg was useless and that the building in which he was had been set on fire. In great pain he managed to crawl past some Egyptians who did not kill him. At last light, waving a white handkerchief, he was seen and rescued by Malcolm Elliott and Horace McLelland, the padre, who had gone up to help boost morale.

Great was the rejoicing by his comrades and the morale of the whole battalion soared at the news of his safe return alive.

I have said very little about the Sappers so far but this is not because they were not doing anything. Jock Brazier and his men were very busy doing many dirty, difficult and dangerous jobs such as clearing mines, repairing the road, water supplies, etc.

One of the dirty ones was the lugubrious business of dealing with the corpses. In this connection a curious event took place.

During the day a group of people was seen coming down the road out of Port Said. They were a party of mourners complete with a coffin. In spite of all that was going on they insisted on burying the body in the cemetery. A macabre event, as the place was littered with bodies.

We never did meet up with the Marines that day. Fighting their way through the town had proved more difficult than expected. There were the inevitable delays in getting the troops ashore and 2 Para, who were to lead the advance south, were not able to link up with their tanks until dark. By this time it had been officially ordered that there was to be a 'Cease Fire' at 2359hrs when all movement must stop.

Tubby Butler characteristically attached himself to the leading troops as they fought their way out of Port Said and dashed down the Canal road. At midnight they were nowhere in particular so he insisted on going on to the next Canal Station. About 0200hrs 2 Para Group reached El Cap where they had to stop. He could do no more.

The main reason for this was the clever sabre-rattling by the Russians. They demanded immediate cessation of hostilities and alluded to 'Russian atomic missiles which could reach London and Paris'. World opinion, especially in USA, was against us and, coupled with this veiled threat, was enough to compel the British and French to stop.

I remembered vividly that night listening to this in our 'brothel' on the edge of Port Said and feeling that although militarily it was obvious that we should go on and take the Canal we could not risk starting an atomic war. To stop would mean that all our efforts and sacrifices would be in vain. But this was to come later and there was a small war going on. For we were still on our own and although we observed the 'Cease Fire' the Egyptians certainly did not and firing went on throughout the night.

At dawn Egyptian armed troops were found to be still holding the buildings near the hospital at the road junction. However, later in the morning they were quietly eased out, the road to the docks opened, and the link up effected with the Royal Marines. A patrol from 1 Para also joined us along the beaches.

I met the Allied Commander-in-Chief, General Sir Charles Keightley, when he landed on El Gamil airfield and showed him the scene of our battles. Having sent us off on our own he was very relieved that things had gone so well and was very complimentary about the parachutists. He was then joined by General 'Hughie' Stockwell and some senior RAF officers. So Stan Roe had to relinquish the post of Senior Air Officer Port Said.

Most of the Battalion Group moved up into a reasonable area further into Port Said and came under command of the Commando Brigade and genial Brigadier Rex Maddox. We were given a sector and the task of maintaining law and order in it.

Our sector included the area over which we had fought and ironically we now set about putting it together again. We were careful not to inflict any further damage. I was livid when I found soldiers of a Regiment, which shall remain nameless, who had been temporarily billeted in our area wantonly destroying furnishings and fittings in the flats. The Egyptian soldiers had made use of these flats against us. But once we had cleared them out we were careful to preserve them for their rightful occupants. We harboured no ill feeling or resentment against Egyptian civilians. To see this unnecessary damage being laughingly perpetrated by people who had not fought was infuriating. Some of the relieving units were also very 'trigger happy'. It did no good to the name of the British Army and we were inevitably but wrongly associated with it.

We were occupied in clearing up the native quarter, collecting arms, enforcing the curfew and the like. We worked in co-operation with a troop of 6 Royal Tanks also using our own 'tank'. This was one of the captured Russian SU 100s armoured tracked vehicles with a gun, which was virtually a tank.

Sergeant Turkiewitz, who had fought with an armoured regiment in the war, got one in working order and very capably drove me around. We put 3 Para markings on it and it became known as 'Crook's tank'. We lost it when we left Port Said but it is now in the tank museum at Bovington where the faint 3 Para markings can still just be seen.

The Sappers worked extremely hard and their worst task was the disposal of corpses which had to be done quickly, and they poured out to the cemetery in all sorts of transport. There were masses of bodies of all ages and sexes. Who caused all these deaths we did not know but it certainly was not us. There were so many that they had to be buried in bulldozed mass graves.

The 1st Battalion of my former Regiment, the Queen's Own Royal West Kent Regiment, were part of the assault force and it was a great pleasure to be able to render them some assistance. In the way things were, their transport came ashore twenty-four hours before their main body. So I took them under my wing and found them an assembly area in my limited parish using a school on the beaches. It was a great joy for me when the next day standing on my tank I watched my old friends march past. They were to take over from 2 Para at El Cap and I was able to give the CO, Peter Buckle, the form and take care of the 2i/c, Bobby Flint, and the rest whilst in the assembly area.

On Friday 'A' Company Group was ordered up to the canal station at El Tina as a long stop to 2 Para facing the enemy at El Cap some miles ahead. The main excitement here occurred when Mike Walsh was discovered *en deshabille* at siesta

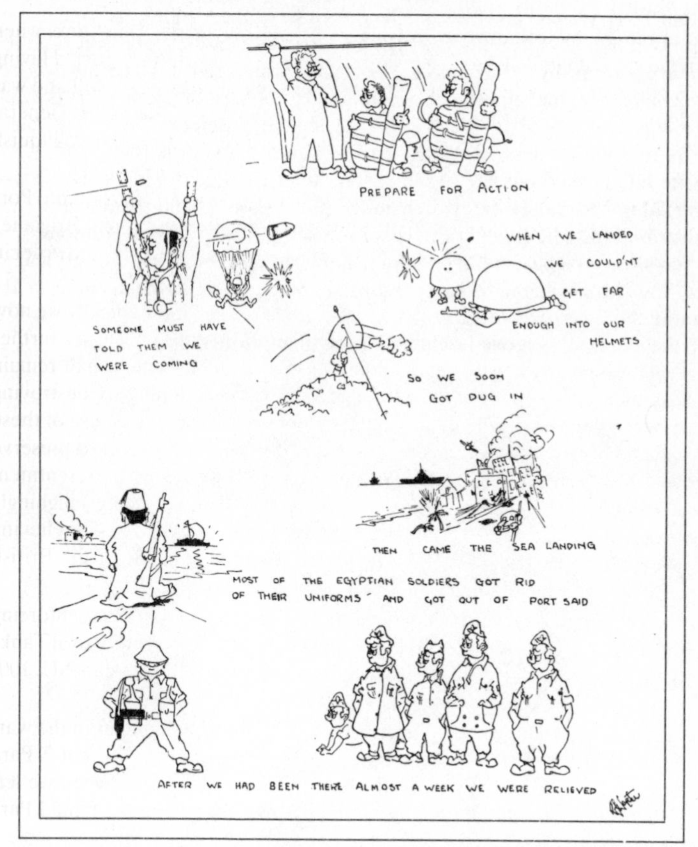

By courtesy of *Pegasus*, Journal of the Parachute Regiment Airborne Forces.

time by an attractive French lady journalist. I went down the Canal to visit 'A' Company at El Tina and see my friends at El Cap. Driving back in the dark in a car with very poor lights was a dicey business as the road was pitted with unforeseeable shell holes. But thanks to the skill of my driver, Norman Bishop, we managed to survive.

This was not the same for four officers led by Tony Watson. Their jeep crashed and although unhurt they ended up in a small canal alongside the road. Was this the Sweet Water Canal? It so it was full of *bilharzia*. Apparently it was not, as four worried officers never suffered any ill effects.

Sunday was Remembrance Sunday and Horace McLelland conducted a dignified service on the airfield at which we remembered our own dead.

For a few happy hours it was officially stated that we were to embark on the *New Australia* on Monday and sail straight back home aboard her. Embark on the Monday we did, but only to return to Cyprus.

One final operational point.

It should be clear from this narrative of events in Port Said that our communications worked well. As indeed they did, and great credit is due to Captain Tony Watson and his signallers. As a start, the load they carried in their weapons container was quite horrific. But there was a bit more to it than just efficient operating by the signallers. The right sets are needed. I have always been a great believer in the importance of communications and of taking every possible step to ensure they work properly. Thus during the summer in Cyprus I managed to acquire some wireless sets which worked better than our normal issue. When Brigade HQ arrived out late in the proceedings, the senior administrative staff officer, Major Farrar-Hockley, demanded that I should hand them over to him for distribution as he thought fit. This I refused to do for obvious reasons; they had become a vital part of our communication set-up. They were our sets and we knew how to use them. What is more we were going to need them in the operation.

In the event I was proved right and more than justified.

20
Suez: The Aftermath

Makin' mock o' uniforms that guard you while you sleep – Kipling

For a day on board the *New Australia* we were rather pleased with ourselves. Perhaps too pleased: but, after all, we had as the sole British Army unit, with support from the other two Services, achieved the following: The capture of an airfield which could be used four hours after we landed. The clearing of the Egyptian forces from the airfield east to the outskirts of Port Said town. The prevention of any enemy reinforcements coming in from the west. The capture of major items of equipment in addition to many small arms and similar weapons.

The Prime Minister had described it as 'a military feat unparallelled in history'.

The cost: four dead and thirty-five seriously wounded.

We did not know then the sort of reception we were to receive both in Cyprus and UK.

We arrived off Famagusta at dawn but we were not allowed to disembark at Limassol until late afternoon. By then a reception party consisting solely of a Military Police Officer and some Red Caps (Military Police) was awaiting us. Everyone else was too busy it seemed.

The Provost officer informed me that he intended to search us for weapons. I watched for a while as my battle-experienced soldiers were subjected to a humiliating total body search by raw, unseasoned military personnel who had never seen a shot fired in anger. The sight of my men being treated as common criminals became too much for me and I exploded. I ordered it to stop. The Provost officer remonstrated insisting that the searching had to go on. I refused to allow it and said that I would take the consequences.

I was told later that some French Paras who had arrived back in Cyprus before us had brought some Egyptian weapons with them and had sold them to EOKA, the Cypriot terrorist movement. Now, it was true that although we had left most of our captured equipment and weapons behind us we had brought some with us so that we could show how much better they were than our own. We certainly were not going to sell them to EOKA but rather use them against EOKA. We had been fighting EOKA for nearly a year and the idea of our helping them in any way was ludicrous.

But there was no one there to support me at the time and I had defied the might of the Provost machine, a dangerous thing to do. I more or less got away with it but it was not forgotten and we featured in their black books. The soldiers rallied round and concealed the weapons cleverly until we got home when we displayed them quite openly.

After this 'welcome' it was back to Tunisia Camp where we set about planning to carry out another parachuted operation if required. It was not, and suddenly we were sent home for Christmas. Here again a very mixed reception awaited us.

Ironically it started with the plane carrying me and the advance party ending up at the wrong airfield at Southend-on-Sea where no one expected us.

Naturally our families and, to be fair, Aldershot were pleased to see us. But the country in general greeted us unenthusiastically. We were associated with unnecessary death and destruction in Port Said and the introduction of petrol rationing.

As time went by the ill-informed criticism and ill-feeling got worse. The word Suez came to be associated with incompetence and failure politically and militarily. Politically it may well have been a disaster and it is not for me to comment on that. But that is no reason to classify the military operation as a fiasco as it has long been fashionable so to do. It was far from being a military failure.

The main military criticism is of the time which elapsed after the air attack on the Egyptian Air Force and the arrival of the ground forces. It is true that this did happen but the reason is political not military. When the Israelis started their attack on Egypt the Allied Commander-in-Chief was given a political order to start the allied attack. He could not choose his own time for 'H' hour but had to accept the political one. He had ten hours' notice instead of the accepted ten days.

The disposition of his amphibious forces at the time of being given the order to go was such that it would take six days' sailing to reach Egypt and nothing could be done about that.

A commander before a big battle makes sure that all his forces are in the right place and then selects his own time, 'H' hour, to start it.

Left to himself the C-in-C, General Keightley, would have set off his amphibious force timed to arrive to exploit closely the air assault, not four days later. The successful destruction of the enemy's air forces was achieved even more quickly than expected, making the time lag appear even greater.

Another political decision prevented him from using the Armoured Division stationed in Libya which could have exploited the situation more effectively.

All this goes to show that there was absolutely no military collusion with the Israelis whatever the political state of play, as subsequently disclosed, may have been.

General Keightley was essentially a loyal soldier who obeyed orders. He carried out the instructions of his political masters to the letter even if in this case it did no good to his high reputation. He never 'moaned' or 'wrote a book about it' (as I am now doing). Even his final Despatch was politically censored and he did confide in me that he wished he had been able to say more.

As for the actual conduct of the operation, it was far from a failure. The Royal Navy and Royal Air Force acquitted themselves admirably throughout. The drops and actions by Parachute troops have been accepted as being most efficient and successful. The landings by amphibious forces were competently carried out.

That there was some mistakes and hiccups was only natural. Some of these hiccups, such as the arrival of an officers' mess truck without the officers, received far more attention than normal because after the 'Cease Fire' the spotlight was turned on them. Such things do happen in a combined amphibious operation mounted from various places.

I was actively involved in 'Operation Zipper', the amphibious assault on the beaches of Malaya. It had all the advantages of wartime experience and equipment and yet in my opinion was much less well-planned and executed than 'Operation Musketeer'.

No, Her Majesty's Armed Forces in Egypt in November 1956 have no reason to be ashamed of themselves.

Other criticisms: the damage; yes, it was considerable, but most of it was caused by the refusal of Cairo to allow the Egyptian military commander on the spot to surrender after the parachute landings the first day.

The deaths; an appalling number which was never correctly estimated. But many of them were undoubtedly perpetrated by the inhabitants of Port Said themselves, thanks in no small measure to the indiscriminate hand-out of weapons by the Russian Consul.

The medical situation; first, we did absolutely no harm to the hospital or its patients as was outrageously stated by an ignorant, prejudiced Labour lady Member of Parliament. At best, the place was pretty awful and without staff a shambles. We were sorry for the patients and offered help which was rejected. The Para Field Ambulance set up an emergency casualty station in the Fruit Market where they operated on several hundred Egyptians.

Equipment; a different story and no criticism can be too strong. It starts with the aeroplanes and carries right through to the soldier's personal weapon. There were very few transport aircraft and they were out of date. There was also a lack of proper air delivery equipment including the parachutist's clumsy weapons container. Those who dropped with the French noted with envy the marked contrast between their light, easily handled equipment and our own. The British parachutist was angry on arrival in Egypt to find that the average Egyptian soldier was better armed than himself. We threw away our ineffective Sten guns and used their light automatics.

Lastly, 'having started, why didn't you go on?'

'Well, we received a signal telling us to stop.'

'But couldn't you have done a Nelson and turned a blind eye to this signal?'

'General Hughie Stockwell was astute enough to guess something like that might possibly happen. So he sent his senior liaison officer, a parachutist, to Brigadier Tubby Butler with a copy of the signal. Tubby could never say he hadn't got it. As it was he went on for two hours longer than permitted to reach the canal station at El Cap, with the liaison officer breathing down his neck. Given another twenty-four hours we might have finished the job. But the politicians couldn't or wouldn't allow this.'

'But don't blame us.'

My abiding memory is of the courage and resolution of the young parachute soldier who went forward regardless and made it look so easy in retrospect, which it certainly was not at the time.

There is one happy aftermath.

Nasser claimed that he had wiped out the British parachute battalion which jumped at Port Said and that 'the Suez Canal ran red with their blood'!

However, twenty years later there were still some of us around who had survived this fate.

There was always a unique spirit in the 3 Para Group which has bound us together ever since. It cannot be defined or explained but probably springs from the shared feeling of pride in having taken part together in a parachute jump against an active enemy and won. Anyway, it gives rise to a feeling that we should like to see each other again and recall the happenings.

Thus on Friday 5 November 1976 a dinner was held in Browning Barracks, Aldershot, to celebrate the 20th anniversary of the Parachute Assault on El

Gamil Airfield by the 3rd Parachute Battalion Group on 5 November 1956. It had been difficult to get in touch with everybody but of the 700 odd who jumped at Suez nearly 100 attended, including our French liaison officer, François Collet, and one non-jumper, the gallant pilot of the French Dakota which landed so early in the proceedings, Colonel de Fourquières. People came from places as far away as Germany, Cyprus and even Canada.

Thanks to the organisation by Gerald Mullins it proved a great success and there was a strong demand for another one. So five years later the 25th anniversary was celebrated, well organised by Jim Burke. This time over 100 attended.

Next, Geoff Norton was prevailed upon to organise the 30th Anniversary Dinner. Although time moves on, the spirit is still there and a total of 111 turned up from all over the world. This included four Generals, two Brigadiers, six Colonels, a Captain of industry and a French Senateur, as well as many other distinguished citizens: not bad going. I was able to point out in my speech 'I must have trained you lot pretty well'!

Major Brian Sharman has undertaken to organise the next one. It is no easy task but very worthwhile as it brings a lot of happiness and satisfaction to a small body of men who took part together in what is a very tiny item of military history and yet never forgotten by them.

21
Airborne Development

No idea is so outlandish that it should not be considered with a searching but at the same time with a steady eye – Winston Churchill

I had the distinction of commanding 3 Para for another year. Though I say it myself, we were a cracking good battalion, the best. Experienced, efficient and enthusiastic, all ranks could and did do anything I asked of them. We were to prove this publicly when, in October, we were lent to 3 Division for their exercise 'Autumn Flight'. We were part of the famous Chindit Bernard Fergusson's Brigade.

We hung around doing nothing at the Warminster end of Salisbury Plain for twenty-four hours. His other battalions were bogged down and he had to launch us. We broke out and, using improved forms of transport, doubled across the Plain and bounced the river-crossing places before anyone was ready for us. Then, foregoing sleep, we put in a properly conducted night attack and captured Sidbury Hill at dawn, thus achieving the object of the exercise. The Divisional Commander, Major-General Gordon Lennox, was very magnanimous, and agreed that our actions had been correctly carried out and ended his exercise thirty-six hours earlier than planned. Afterwards he was openly most congratulatory. Some time later the Adjutant, Karl Beale, was on a Company Commanders' Course at the School of Infantry and heard our performance described as a model of how a battalion should be handled and operate: proudly he was able to say, 'Well, that was my battalion.'

Throughout, we were madly busy as a Parachute battalion always is, alternating between Guards of Honour in Aldershot and parachuted exercises all over the place.

Highlights included a visit by His Royal Highness, The Duke of Gloucester, who came to see and hear about our exploits at Port Said. He was very interested and most gracious. We like to think that he enjoyed his lunch, as did the officer standing in for him on the rehearsal! He was closely followed by the Secretary of State for War, Mr John Hare.

A ceremonial event was the presentation of the Freedom of the Borough of Aldershot to the Parachute Regiment. I have always disliked ceremonial and, not being Sandhurst trained, I was not very good at it. For this occasion I was taken quietly to one side by the Regimental Sergeant Major, John Lord, and put through my paces until I was a credit to the Battalion.

We studied the lessons learned in our parachute action at Port Said and played our part in helping to improve the development of airborne equipment and techniques. An unusual way of doing this was to recreate the drop onto El Gamil airfield in a television programme. During that summer the BBC produced a series of programmes called 'Now'. They went out live, depicting events happening at the time of showing. Each of the Services, including the Army, did one and ours was an extra, almost unnoticed at first. It was produced by BBC Wales. Mike Walsh was virtually the scriptwriter and assistant producer and did an outstanding job. Raymond Baxter and I were the commentators.

The scenario was very similar to Port Said. We jumped onto and captured the disused airfield at Aberporth, having taken off from the Royal Naval Air Station at Brawdy. TV zero hour was at half-past-seven on what happily turned out to be a fine summer evening. Timings for this live programme had to be absolutely spot on which, thanks to the RAF, they were. There were cameras everywhere including two inside a Beverly aircraft showing the parachutists as they went out, which was new and quite dramatic. A parachutist took a camera and microphone with him and talked himself down to the ground. Some of the action on the ground had, of course, to take place in front of the camera regardless of what was happening to the parachutists. These episodes were produced in accordance with the script, including one of me dressed as a parachutist taking command. Needless to say, I had not arrived by air but most of the others had!

The family at home saw all this live as it happened and it made some exciting viewing. Candidly it was much better than the rather dull Army programme. Much later I gathered that, far from being pleased, the Army hierarchy were rather annoyed.

To mark the retirement from the Army of General Sir Charles Keightley he took the salute at a Beating of Retreat by the Band and Drums. Bandmaster Crossman included two swinging marching numbers in the programme – *The Saint Louis Blues* and *The Saints Go Marching In*. The soldiers actually applauded, a thing they were not normally given to doing at a Retreat. It had my approval, but again not that of some of the hierarchy.

Anyway, it was time for me to be put in my place and to be sent to Coventry, or to be more accurate, Shrewsbury, where I was appointed the General Staff Officer Grade 1 at Headqurters Midwest District. Happily, the GOC was an outstanding officer called Lewis Pugh and we got on very well together.

Although the District included two Territorial Army Divisions, one Welsh, one Midland, and two Civil Defence Areas based on Cardiff and Birmingham, the General and I usually managed two days a week off, he at his home near Machynlleth in Wales and I playing cricket. It is perhaps impertinent to note that there are now two Generals and staffs where we only needed one.

The cricket was good: I ran the Comand side with a very good fixture list. Our team included National Servicemen Alan Jones, later the Glamorgan opening bat, and Norman Gifford of Worcestershire and England.

Driving home from a match one evening in a humble Austin 7 I went round a bend and found a van coming straight at me on my side of the road. 'Hell,' I thought, 'if he doesn't move I've had it.' He didn't, and although I swerved across the road at the last second, he struck my nearside good and hard. Fortunately there was no passenger, but as for me, when I came to I found myself in a ditch with a person leaning over me saying: 'I am a Dutchman, I am very sorry I forget which side of the road to drive on.'

No, I was not hallucinating, he was indeed a Dutchman who had driven his truck out of a farm up the road and had forgotten to drive on the left. I have done the same thing myself driving on the Continent but got away with it. Meanwhile I had only partly got away with this, as my left shoulder and knee were severely damaged and I had to sample the delights of hospitals at Bridgnorth and Wolverhampton before recovering.

However, I did not have to spend too long in the pleasant western countryside and next year, to my delight, was promoted and posted to command The Army Airtransport Training and Development Centre (AATDC) located at RAF Old Sarum, near Salisbury.

This establishment did what its cumbersome title implied, that is to say it was responsible for developing the techniques of delivering equipments by air into battle (not peacetime air movement) and then teaching people how to use them. I had experts in every field of airborne delivery on my staff and it was a fascinating and exciting business. My job was to draw up priorities and try to ensure that the experts followed them. On the training side I was more at home and could play an active part. I developed some lectures which people seemed to find interesting. Certainly they were in popular demand and involved me in trips to Canada, Cyprus, Libya, Singapore and Malaya, and North-West Europe: not bad going.

RAF Old Sarum was a delightful Station. It housed the School of Land Air Warfare with whom we worked very closely and the Commandants, Air Vice-Marshals Donald Evans and 'Ginger' Weir, were always most gracious and helpful. It also boasted the best Service Officers' Mess in Britain even if the mess manager did eventually run off with some of the funds!

Of our many activities in my time perhaps the most exciting and demanding was the production of an item for the Royal Tournament at Olympia. This consisted of an airborne assault into battle and involved dropping not only parachutists but also an anti-tank gun and vehicle on a platform by parachute from the roof into the arena at Olympia. Parachutists had been done before and were comparatively easy but the gun was another matter and demanded a great deal of technical skill. This was brilliantly taken care of by our REME Officer, Major Mick Hunt, and his team. We used the old airstrip hangar at Cardwell for rehearsals. Climbing around the roof was a hair-raising experience.

Major David Callaghan, a signaller turned infantryman, looked after the action on the ground, which included a short mock battle. He was a stout-hearted chap and carried on even after the dropped platform had bounced into him. Putting on this performance twice daily for nearly three weeks was a demanding and exhausting business. I was there every night and met all the distinguished visitors who were full of praise, but I never felt we got the credit we deserved either from the organisers or the Regiment.

A perk which we enjoyed was to be invited by firms to their pavilion at the Farnborough Air Show. The problem was how to make the best use of all the hospitality offered. I solved this by partaking of the smoked salmon in one place, the steak in the next, strawberries and cream in the last and liquid refreshment in all. Needless to say, I did not drive myself!

Among the many overseas visitors to Old Sarum there came my old friend from the Staff Colleges at Leavenworth and Camberley, Bill Yarborough. He was now a General and concerned with forming the US Army Special Airborne Forces. He was very glad to see me and genuinely interested in what we had to show him. He rose to the top of the US Army.

In the development field we continued to clear aerial delivery loads from the Beverley. We also started on loads from the splendid American transport plan the C 130 which happily the RAF were soon to purchase. Regrettably we also played a small part in the development of the Argosy, a terrible transport plane designed like a camel by committee with a hump.

My own pet projects were for the benefit of the parachutist.

First there was a replacement parachute which let him down more gently. It could only be done at the expense of losing some manoeuvrability in the air. It was a choice between a sports car and a saloon. I favoured the latter.

Next came a simple means of training parachutists. For this Walter Neumark, a leading expert in aerial techniques, produced a 'kite' parachute, *ie* an ascending parachute. It was put onto the parachutist on the ground and he was fixed by cable to a land rover which drove forward and caused the parachutist to rise into the air. At a suitable moment he detached the cable and descended to the ground in the normal way. This could possibly have done away with much of the expensive training by the RAF. This would never do and it was never adopted, but it has since become a popular civilian sport.

My other hobby horse was a flying bicycle invented and successfully demonstrated by a Wing-Commander Wallis. I believe it would have been invaluable in enabling a front line commander both to move about and to see 'over the hill'. But it has never found much favour. For that matter new items which did find favour often took as along as twenty years before they went into service. Such is the tempo of development by Whitehall Committee.

Every day at the AATDC was full of interest and action. In addition to the work, we ran a hockey team which reached the final of the Army Minor Units Hockey Competition and were only narrowly beaten by Mons Officer Cadet Training unit, a bogus minor unit. Cricket was good too. Nevertheless I began to get worried as to what I was going to do next.

The out of the blue came a posting order sending me to Jamaica to take charge of their Defence Forces after Independence. This was to be granted quite soon and there was no time to be lost for me to get there before the ceremony took place.

22
Jamaica

I am for the West. I am against anything that has the semblance of Communism – Sir Alexander Bustamante

I arrived at Palisadoes airport, Kingston, Jamaica twenty-four hours late after another alarming flight. Rupert, my Dachshund, and I left Heathrow in a plane which should have taken us all the way to Jamaica via New York, I in a first-class cabin seat, Rupert in a crate in the hold. It was important not to change planes as if Rupert put so much as one paw on foreign soil he would not be allowed into Jamaica because of rabies.

However, about two hours short of New York our plane ran into a terrific storm and was struck by lightning. Much of the electrical equipment ceased to function and we eventually staggered into Baltimore. This was a great relief and all right for me but not so for Rupert stuck in the hold on a very hot afternoon. After a lot of hassle I managed to get him transferred direct to another plane which it was said would eventually take us to Jamaica. But we still had to go via New York, where I spent a night in luxury at the Saint Regis Hotel and Rupert in his crate.

I had to settle down very quickly in what were unfamiliar but never unfriendly circumstances and take part in the Independence Ceremony on 6 August 1962. It was very well done and had been masterminded by Colonel Eric Heffer, who had become the acknowledged expert in the business of hauling down the Union Jack. Her Royal Highness Princess Margaret represented Her Majesty the Queen, and Vice President Lyndon Johnson the United States of America.

Thereafter I was to take an active part in the formative years of the newly independent State of Jamaica. As Chief of Staff of the Jamaica Defence Force I was *de facto* in command of all the armed forces. I was responsible for the defence and security of the Island and was a member of the Defence Board. Officially I came under the direction of the Minister of Home Affairs, Roy McNeil, but in practice I soon found that I worked direct to the Prime Minister, Sir Alexander Bustamante.

'Busta', as he liked to be known, was an outstanding personality, in some respects a sort of cross between Lloyd George and Ernest Bevin. He had had an astonishing career about which a large, fascinating book could be written. Born in Jamaica, he went as a youth to Spain where it is said he served as a Cavalry Officer in the Spanish Army. Subsequently he became an Inspector in the Havana Police Force, Cuba. For some years he worked as a dietician in a hospital in New York and made money on the stock market there. Then in the 30s he returned to his native Jamaica and embarked on a turbulent career in politics, founding a Trades Union and a Political Party. Like all the best anti-Colonial leaders, he was locked up by the British but now was the leader of his independent country, respected by all.

Happily he took to me and I became devoted to him and his competent and charming wife, Gladys.

I also rapidly became firm friends with the Commissioner of Police, Noel Crosswell, with whom I worked very closely.

Although concerned in detail with all aspects of the Defence Force I also often operated at what I can describe in all honesty as a very high level.

For instance, I persuaded Sir Alexander that Jamaica should play a military part in the United Nations Organisation and offer a contribution, however modest, to any UN military force. U Thant paid a visit to Jamaica and later I visited him at UN Headquarters in New York. There I completed the details with his military staff. We could only produce a company group but that was better than nothing. It was also good for the Jamaica Regiment, as it gave them an interest and role other than just the defence of the country and ceremonial at which they were very good.

Another example of my diverse levels of operating concerned Canada who took on the role of 'Big Brother' to young Jamaica. I went twice to Ottawa where I discussed with the Canadian Chief of Defence Staff, Air Chief Marshal Miller, an agreement for the exchange of troops for training. I then went down the corridor and saw a staff captain to arrange a course in Canada for a Jamaican Cadet.

Not long after independence came the missile crisis in Cuba which brought considerable benefits to the Jamaica Defence Force. Many of the Caribbean and South American countries went cap in hand to USA for hand-outs. We did not need to do this as Cuba proved that Jamaica had something that the US Forces needed, namely the use of Kingston harbour.

I suggested to the Prime Minister that he should not give them this facility *carte blanche* but should bargain for something in return. Having been American staff trained I knew the right catch words to influence the Pentagon and asked for 'a recon capability'.

I explained to the Americans that with only two battalions we could not expect to defend the whole island against an invasion but we would like to be able to know when and where it was coming and so be able to ask for help. To do this the Jamaica Defence Force needed to be able to watch its coast on the sea and in the air. Specifically I asked for and got three patrol boats, four light aircraft and a dozen armed jeeps for a reconnaissance platoon.

Negotiations took some time but eventually we reached an agreement and took delivery of all this ironmongery.

I also purchased two small Bell helicopters. This was early days for helicopters and they cost no more each than an expensive car. Bells gave us a free course for the pilots and they managed to get to Jamaica by judicous island-hopping through the Bahamas, a considerable feat.

The Air Wing was organised and trained by Major Whittingham-Jones who was a brilliant, fearless pilot on both fixed and rotary wing aircraft. Once, he took off from our small strip in Up Park Camp in a tropical storm to casevac a sick person from the Cayman Islands. We were very relieved when he returned safely from this dangerous mercy mission.

The Lemoigne parascending chute was obtained from UK and I 'persuaded' two British seconded officers to make some flights. Altogether the Air Wing could put on quite a good little display which it successfully did to impress both the public and politicians.

A Sea Squadron was also formed under the supervision of Lieutenant-Commander J. Bailey, RN and the first of three boats commissioned by Lady Bustamante at a handing-over ceremony by the US Navy.

So the Jamaica Defence Force in my time became one of the first joint Forces, all ranks having the same basic uniform and titles. Some members of the Sea Squadron were not too pleased at first, and when Admiral Lord Louis Mountbatten came to pay us a visit tried to lobby him to make me allow them to become a separate Navy. I accepted that when at sea they could, say, wear and do whatever was appropriate for their nautical role but that fundamentally they must be members of the Jamaica Defence Force. Although a great protagonist of 'jointery' I don't think the Admiral entirely approved!

Meetings with the Prime Minister often ended with a private champagne session which helped to cement our mutual regard. A measure of the bigness of the man and our relationship is illustrated by an episode at a Defence Board meeting. We were considering promotions of senior police officers. The name of 'X' was tentatively put forward for one of the top posts. Silence.

Having seen a little of him in action and finding him pretty good, I blithely stepped in and recommended him. There were intakes of breath and looks of apprehension among the other members. Suddenly 'Busta' said, 'Well Brig, if you think he's good enough he can have the job.'

Unknown to me, this officer had once arrested 'Busta' none too gently and flung him into prison.

Ignorance is bliss.

It was noised around that perhaps I had the ear of the Prime Minister and I was lobbied by various parties, including the United States Ambassador. Visits were arranged to the neighbouring US Commands and I was invited on board US Navy ships, such as aircraft carriers, when anchored in Kingston harbour. This was not as much fun as it might seem as it involved considerable ceremonial in best uniform on hot flight decks. Since they were 'dry' ships, afterwards one was only revived by 'Coke'.

The first visit was to the American Forces in the island of Puerto Rico. At San Juan the Commander was Major-General Roland Del Mar who showed me round and entertained us most hospitably. His house was very old, having been built not long after the time of Christopher Colombus. He very kindly presented me with a swagger stick made out of the original wood, which was very strong. We called on His Excellency the Governor and visited the Naval Base as well as Army units. It was good value as a friendly liaison visit.

Next I went to Panama as the guest of Lieutenant-General Andrew P. O'Meara, Commander-in-Chief Caribbean Command. This visit was most important, as technically Jamaica came within his sphere of influence and he could do much for us. I made a number of useful contacts in the Canal Zone. But the most practical and entertaining visit was to the Jungle Warfare Training Centre at the other end of the Canal, where I spent nearly a day.

They taught how to survive in the jungle and having been to a Jungle Warfare School in Malaya I could hold my own. But I had to admit that whereas the jungle in Malaya is neutral, in South America it most certainly is not, being full of many horrible, hostile creatures.

. The last session consists of being shown slides of life in the jungle. As one looks to the front at these, an instructor creeps up behind and puts a 'tame' boa constrictor round one's neck. Some people may not mind but I could not bear the idea. In this I was at one with the late Robert Kennedy who refused to have the creature put on him. Alert to this, I turned round just in time and said: 'I agree with your Attorney General. I will not have that thing on me.'

This caused some consternation, as a picture of oneself with a boa round one's neck qualified one for a handsome certificate as an Honorary Jungle Expert. One had been prepared in my name. I steadfastly refused to change my mind but said I was willing to have my picture taken with any other jungle creature they liked other than a reptile.

'OK,' they said, 'will you have it taken with a puma?'

'Certainly,' I replied.

So I was wheeled off to the puma's cage and there had my picture taken patting its head. It looked quite docile to me and I was not particularly concerned. But I was told afterwards that its temper was very unpredictable and much more dangerous than a boa constrictor. Anyway, honour was satisfied and I was awarded my Jungle Certificate!

Finally I was asked by Rear-Admiral James W. Davis to visit him at the US Naval Base at Guantanamo in Cuba and he sent a naval plane to fetch me.

Guantanamo base is on permanent lease from Cuba and consists of forty-five square miles, one third of which is water. The bay is a fine harbour and it is an excellent centre for training by the Atlantic Fleet. When I was there the total American population was nearly 10,000. Admiral Davis was a distinguished submariner and great fun. He took me on a personally conducted tour of the whole base and its defences. We also had a whale of a party at the Officers' Club.

Mrs Davis gave a lunch party before we left in the afternoon. So far, there had never been any salt on the table which I miss very much. Sitting on her right I felt that after last night's festivities I knew her well enough by now to venture to ask for some salt. But I was mistaken: a beautiful friendship flew out of the window.

'Oh, General,' (we had been on Christian name terms) 'hasn't my cooking been salt enough for you?'

'Of course, it's been lovely,' I lamely replied, 'it's just that I particularly like some extra with lobster.' (Or whatever it was we were eating).

The Philippino steward was sent to fetch some salt. After a long pause he appeared with a silver salt-cellar. Under the beady eye of my hostess I proceeded to shake it. For a while nothing happened and then suddenly the top fell off and my plate was covered with salt!

But this was not the end of my social calamities.

In the way one does in an English house I left some change on the dressing table as a present for the servants. I was just about to review a Guard of Honour which had been graciously provided by the Marines, when the house steward came running up and in front of all presented me with this money saying: 'You left this behind, Sir.'

Not unnaturally I have never been back to Guantanamo, but the US Navy is still there.

The United Kingdom did not neglect us and I was bidden by the Chief of the Defence Staff, Admiral Mountbatten, and the Chief of the Imperial General Staff, General Hull, to attend their Exercises at Dartmouth and Camberley. The Jamaican Permanent Secretary for Defence, B.St.J. Hamilton, an admirable fellow, went with me. As well as taking part in these high powered exercises, we did a lot of business with various departments in Whitehall.

The next year I went by myself to the CIGS's exercise and once again was extremely busy. But it was great fun to be at Camberley as a guest and to be able to offer drinks to my elders and betters without cost to myself. Not that it did me much good.

Although I kept in close touch with the UK High Commissioner, Sir Alexander Morley, I was not a member of his staff, having been loaned to the Jamaican Government without strings. It meant that I did not have a confidential report for three years during a period when they might even have been rather good ones. I did not bother about it at the time, not appreciating that it upset the Military Secretary's Department and would probably cost me dear.

Life was not all exotic expeditions, as might appear so far. There was a great deal of military work to be done in forming the new Defence Force. In addition to the infantry, administrative support units had to be formed to perform duties which had previously been carried out by British units. This called for specialist experience not always readily available. To assist, I had a team of some twenty British officers and a dozen senior non-commissioned officers. They were replaced by Jamaicans as and when available. Like me, they belonged to the Jamaican Government and only had me to look after their interests. There were some problems and before leaving I arranged that our successors were attached to the UK High Commission as a military training team acting as advisors to the Defence Force without any command functions.

The new units, including the naval and air ones, required recruits in all ranks and equipment obtained. We had a small training Depot up in the Blue Mountains behind Kingston at Newcastle. It had been set up by the British Army as an escape from the hot coastal plain where so many died of disease. It was a delightful, cool place but took some reaching, up a very winding mountain road. It was a long, tedious journey until reduced to eight minutes by helicopter.

There were Territorial and Cadet units to be encouraged and nurtured in conjunction with the Association Secretary, Brigadier Lindner, a retired Gunner. Here I was very fortunate in that the Commanding Officer of the Territorial Battalion 3JR turned out to be Joe Moody whom I had welcomed into the Royal West Kent Regiment when Adjutant at Maidstone. Joe was head of the Jamaica Transport Company and was most welcoming and helpful; he was also jolly efficient.

The Jamaican soldier is by nature very smart and enjoys putting on a good show on parade. I was concerned with his tactical training and took it upon myself to run study periods and set testing exercises in wild, uninhabited country known as the Cockpit.

It was necessary to keep under review and test emergency plans for hurricanes. It was as well we did as the island was hit by one during the time I was there. We had to be totally battened down for several hours in the camp but did not have the worst of it in Kingston. Some parts of the island were seriously affected with much damage and flooding. We sent military assistance and soon after I accompanied the Prime Minister and Lady Bustamante on a tour of the stricken areas, where we were enthusiastically received.

The Jamaica Legion was a very flourishing concern and one of the best organisations in the island. It was always a pleasure and privilege to go to one of their meetings and functions.

To my surprise I was in considerable demand to attend functions all over the place, varying from children's sports to Legion Dinners. I soon found that no matter what it was there would be speeches and I would be expected to make one. Most of them were rather long and dull, so I endeavoured to make mine short and amusing. I was always on the look-out for new stories and kept a book showing when and where I had told them. This was essential as in a comparatively small society any story once told soon got round and only lasted a few airings.

There was a never-ending stream of visitors. Anyone who possibly could included the Island of Jamaica in his tour itinerary. The military ones were my concern. They are too numerous to name but did include Admiral Mountbatten, as I have already indicated, and the CIGS General Hull; also the American Secretary for Defense, Mr Macnamara, with whom I had a 'working breakfast' beside a swimming pool in Montego Bay. I had to 'field' many others and shield the Prime Minister from them.

Royal visitors were very different. The first was by HRH Princess Margaret accompanied by Lord Snowden. Both were absolutely charming. One recalls a lunch party attended by Noel Coward who had a villa in Jamaica. He never stopped talking and the Princess rarely stopped smoking. It was all very entertaining.

HRH the Princess Alice, Countess of Athlone, was Chancellor of the University of the West Indies which was located near Kingston. She used to come out every year to attend the University's main ceremonies. Although eighty years of age she was very spritely and great fun. She used to like to come up to Newcastle where she scrambled round the steep mountain paths like a ten-year-old.

When Her Majesty the Queen Mother paid a visit to Jamaica she honoured us by spending nearly a day at Newcastle. After lunch she was rather reluctant to tackle the cliff-path walk. Princess Alice was also present and we were tickled to hear her say, 'Come on, Elizabeth, if I can do it you can.' 'Oh, very well, Aunt Alice, if you say so.' And off they went.

The Jamaica Regimental Band and Drums could put on a superb Beating of Retreat. We did one for the Queen Mother on a lovely bright evening on the lawn of Government House with a background of the beautiful Blue Mountains. The Queen Mother was kind enough to say that it was one of the best she had ever seen. I thought so too.

Not least among our many visitors was my good friend Jumbo Courtney. We had been able to see a good deal of each other shortly after the war when we were both in Whitehall. Since then Jumbo had changed partners and occupation. He was now living in Australia with a new family and was successfully building up an import/export agency, dealing primarily with the Middle East. He wondered if he could expand into the West Indies and so turned up in Jamaica.

I managed to get him an interview with the Minister for Trade and Industry and gave him several good introductions but in the end nothing came of it. But it was great to see Jumbo again and we had several good parties including a picnic at Port Royal when we were nearly washed away by a sudden tropical storm.

Because of my liking for cricket and rhythmic music, some people were kind enough to imagine that I had been hand-picked for the job and I did not disillusion them. Not that there was much real jazz, it being the beginning of the reggae era and small groups and there was only one big band. Happily, I sang only very occasionally.

The cricket scene was very different and it was a vintage period. There were several top-class cricketers in the island, the most distinguished being Sir Frank Worrell who was on the faculty of the University of the West Indies. Frank was one of the nicest people I have ever met. A charming gentleman of the highest integrity, he was as fine a statesman off the field as he was outstanding cricketer and sportsman on it. His comparatively early death was a great loss in all respects.

I managed to get my newly formed Defence team accepted into the top club league which was of a very high standard. We held our own the first season, thanks largely to the efforts of a really fast bowler we discovered. He was in the true mould of West Indian fast bowlers and I had high hopes of him following in the footsteps of Wes Hall. But, alas, this was not to be.

One night the big soldier, having enjoyed the favours of a lady of the town refused to pay what she said he owed. She was so incensed that she picked up a pair of scissors and stabbed him. A vital organ was pierced and he died. An unfortunate ending and a big loss.

I was pleased to become a member of Kingston Cricket Club where Alan Rae and Jackie Hendricks, amongst others, were very kind. They organised a special match to celebrate my fiftieth birthday which could be played on the great day in April at Sabina Park.

Religion played a distinct part in life in Jamaica and on Sundays churches were packed with colourful congregations., However, it was accepted that one could take part in sport after one had been to church. I used to take as strong a side as I could muster to play against the large sugar estates and bauxite mines who had grounds of their own and excellent teams. As well as cricket, it was a good way of getting the Force known and understood throughout the island.

I do not smoke myself, having preferred in wartime to swap my cigarette ration for a sweet ration. But I do not wish to prevent anyone from smoking should he wish to do so. In fact I resent the interference by a fanatical minority in the lifestyle of the majority. Anyway, what would cricket have done without the support of the tobacco industry? They certainly supported it in the West Indies in the 60s.

In September 1963 the Machado Tobacco Company (part of the British American Tobacco) brought the whole West Indian team, captained by Frank Worrell, to Jamaica straight from their very successful tour in UK where they won the Test series 3-1. They played two festival matches at Sabina Park and it was a treat to see such cricketers as Sobers, Hunte and Hall in action.

Not to be outdone, Carreras sponsored a team called the Cavaliers to come and play in Jamaica in January 1964. They were captained by Dennis Compton and were nearly all Test players, including Trevor Bailey, Freddie Trueman, Godfrey Evans, amongst others. I arranged for them to play the Force in a friendly game at the Camp.

We batted first and fared reasonably well as Freddie Trueman only bowled at medium pace. However, he suddenly got fed up and clean bowled two batsmen in succession with two very fast deliveries. As I took guard on a hat trick he said, 'Ah, I'm going to fix thee Brig,' and proceeded back to the sight screen. 'Don't worry,' said Godfrey Evans at the stumps behind me, 'he doesn't mean it.' But he did.

Charging flat out, Freddie let one go that was so fast that neither I nor Godfrey saw the ball and it went for 4 byes; the same applied to the next one and then, thankfully, it was over. I made a few runs but before Freddie could attack me again decided to declare.

Freddie's innings was a riot. The ground was packed with spectators, most of them wearing white shirts like the fielders. Coming in at number four Freddie started to enjoy himself hitting a four followed by a six. While the ball was being recovered one of our fielders on the boundary chatted to his mates. Freddie struck the next ball hard and high in his direction. Stepping out of the crowd he made a very good catch. Freddie could not believe it, insisting that he had been caught by a spectator! He returned to the pavilion in a fury muttering something about 'a f'ing, Blo'dy spectator'. It took him some time to recover at the subsequent party we gave for the Cavaliers.

The following January Trevor Bailey brought out another first-class Cavalier side, again sponsored by Carreras. At the same time the Australian Touring Team, captained by Bob Simpson, arrived to play a Test in Jamaica. While the Cavaliers were playing Jamaica at Sabina Park the Australians came and practised at our Camp, which enabled one to meet them all. At a reception we gave for the teams I looked round and saw three lots of the best cricketers in the world all on my lawn, *eg* three great wicket-keepers, Godfrey Evans, Deryck Murray and Wally Grout, and so on. It transpired that Wally Grout was a jazz singer like me and we took turns to entertain the company.

I could go on about cricket but this has probably been more than enough. But I did start by saying it was a vintage period and it is undoubtedly a large part of the West Indian heritage.

So what else? Well there is another episode which might be said to be at a top level as it concerns a Miss World.

The only British Service colleague I had in the Caribbean was called SNOWI – Senior Naval Officer West Indies (not to be confused with SNOW – Senior Naval Officer Wiltshire). He was a Commodore based in Bermuda and used to call on us in a frigate from time to time. During one of these visits we were both invited to be judges in the Competition to choose Miss Jamaica. It boiled down to a choice between two different young ladies. One was beautiful, big, busty and black; the other very pretty, petite and chocolate. The big black girl received the most applause from the audience but I suggested that the small pretty girl was much more the type to do well in the subsequent Miss World Competiton and was strongly supported by SNOWI, Edward Ashmore, thus showing the judgement that was to take him to the summit, Chief of the Defence Staff. In the end our view prevailed and the judges chose our girl as Miss Jamaica. My hunch was right and she did become Miss World.

My contract with the Jamaican Government was for three years. There was talk of extending it, but I knew that was a mistake and it was better to go out on the crest of a wave. So before I was due to leave I handed over to my very competent Deputy, David Smith, and remained for a short while as an advisor.

I had just completed the arrangements for a company from the Jamaica Regiment to carry out an exchange with a company from a British Regiment. I was able to accompany the 1JR Company to UK and so get out of the way for three weeks.

About the same time Busta handed over the post of Prime Minister to his Deputy, the very able and charming Donald Sangster. Sadly, he died soon at early age: another big loss for Jamaica, like that of Frank Worrell. I should mention that as I worked for the Jamaican Government I naturally had most dealings with the members of the party in power. But I was mindful of the need to keep the Leader of the Opposition in the picture about matters concerning the security of his country. He was the statesmanlike Norman Manley, the Hugh Gaitskell of Jamaica, with whom I maintained good relations.

My last main task was to prepare a comprehensive paper for Mr Sangster on the pros and cons of introducing some form of conscription into Jamaica to occupy the unemployed and unruly young men. I was in favour but nothing ever came of it, not surprisingly as it had not long been ended in UK.

And so the time came to leave the lovely island of Jamaica. But before doing so entirely there is one more story of an outside visit which must be told.

It was to the United States of America to President Kennedy's funeral.

23
Funeral of a President

And so, my fellow Americans, ask not what your country can do for you;
ask what can you do for your country – J.F. Kennedy

General Sir Gerald Lathbury, then Quartermaster General of the British Army, was Colonel Commandant of both the Parachute Regiment and the Jamaica Regiment. He took a keen interest in Jamaica and enjoyed his visits, especially the bird-watching expeditions which were carefully planned and laid on by David Smith.

At the end of November 1963 he came out to present new Colours to the 1st Battalion the Jamaica Regiment on Saturday, 23rd.

On Friday, 22 November, came the terrible news of the assassination of President Kennedy. After consultation with the Prime Minister we decided to go ahead with the Presentation Parade the next day. It all went well, and afterwards we were relaxing with a drink when a message came from the Prime Minister saying he had been invited to attend the funeral in Washington on Monday 25th and that he wanted me to go with him.

On the Sunday a party consisting of Sir Alexander and Lady Bustamante; Jimmy Lloyd, his Permanent Secretary; Noel Croswell, Commissioner of Police; and myself, left in a special plane for Washington. Unfortunately we were delayed at Montego Bay, and there was little else we could do during the frustrating wait except revive our spirits with copious quantities of Jamaica's national restorative, the very best rum.

On arrival late in the evening we were met and escorted to the Madison Hotel where we were accommodated in excellent suites with unlimited food and drink.

I must pay tribute to the outstanding arrangements made at very short notice by the American authorities concerned. We were one of many delegations coming from a small island yet we were treated like royalty, which many others attending actually were.

In addition to the accommodation and invitations to the funeral service and other functions, all the arrangements made for us were admirable. We had a security escort and were provided with cars, drivers and motor-cycle outriders. Two motor-cyclists preceded us and swept aside all other traffic, ignoring anything so mundane as traffic lights. It was quite alarming to sit in front with the driver of the leading car and sweep through red lights regardless. The drivers of the bikes were great chaps and quite fearless; they had to be. One equated their chances of survival with those of a subaltern in the First World War.

It intrigued me to see the law-abiding way in which all drivers of other vehicles, on hearing the sirens, promptly pulled into the side of the road and allowed us through. Apparently this facility was enjoyed by all visiting Heads of State. It seemed somewhat undemocratic to me in democratic America.

To return to the funeral. On Monday morning I acompanied Sir Alexander to the White House and we joined the others in the Ballroom. I looked around and found that almost everyone there except me was a Prince, President or Prime Minister.

Sir Alexander and I stood around gloomily for a bit when he was spotted by HRH Prince Philip who came clattering across in his breezy way and said: 'Why, hullo, Busta, this is a very sad occasion, but at least it's good to meet one's friends,' and they chatted away. He also spoke to me and graciously recalled meeting me at Parachute functions. I was relieved to find that his naval funeral uniform agreed with my army version.

He then turned to a little man standing next to me looking very miserable and said in a friendly way: 'And how are you?' Silence, no response. 'Comment vous portez vous?' No response. 'Sprechen sie Deutsch?' Still not the slightest reaction. 'I wonder if he speaks any known language,' said HRH with a smile and moved on to greet someone else. It turned out that the little man was President Enonu of Turkey who had not got his hearing aid switched on!

We then moved out, and on a brisk autumn morning walked in procession from the White House to St Matthew's Cathedral. After the hearse and escort came Mrs Kennedy and family, closely followed by a rank of Princes. We were politely at the rear of the Prime Ministers. Slightly hung over, marching down Connecticut Avenue with members of the Senate breathing down our necks just behind, and flanked by vast silent, grieving crowds it all seemed like a dream.

Inside the Cathedral, Busta and I were seated separately and when the service was over I had to rescue him. There was only one main exit to which the cars of the dignitaries could be brought, one at a time. It was therefore a slow business getting out and we shuffled down the aisle for at least twenty minutes. Tiring for an old man, after a walk.

One was very much aware of the people nearby. From behind came a strong smell of exclusive scent. Glancing round, one encountered Mr Nixon (future President) flanked by two attractive ladies in expensive fur coats. In contrast, next to me, was a small, sinister looking gentleman with side-burns and a pencil moustache, not unlike George Raft. He turned out to be Mr Mikoyan, Deputy President of the Communist Party of the Union of Soviet Republics.

When we at last got back to the Hotel there was just time to get ready to go to a tea party at the White House. All the Kennedys were gathered in welcome and finally one reached Mrs Jacquie Kennedy. My name was announced and she shook me warmly by the hand saying: 'Oh, General, how nice of you to come,' as if she meant it: a remarkable effort.

Finally 'the King is dead, long live the King', and to an evening reception given by President Johnson; dull and very nearly dry.

Quite a day.

The next day we laid a wreath at the grave in a moving little ceremony at Arlington Cemetery. Happily, it was again fine and dry if cold.

It was all over but not the American hospitality. They arranged for us to make a special, private visit to George Washington's estate and home at Mount Vernon, some sixteen miles up the Potomac from Washington. It was interesting to see the Mansion preserved as it used to be in George Washington's time. Sir Alexander and Lady Bustamante were fascinated. I remarked that during our drive to and fro out of town drivers also immediatley fled to the side of the road on the sound of our sirens.

Before we left the Madison, Busta in his inimitable way gave a splendid party for all the people who had looked after us so well. He was a very thoughtful, kindly man. So much so that he next took us all to the Plaza Hotel in New York where we again had a super suite. He gave us two free days which could be spent in luxury there but I preferred to take advantage of the unexpected break to dash over to London to meet someone I very much wanted to see.

Once again my flight across the Atlantic met with trouble and we had to land at Philadelphia. From there I had to take a bus through fog to Idlewild (later Kennedy) Airport. I just managed to scramble into the VIP lounge in time to join the Prime Minister's party before we took off for Jamaica.

24

Aden – The Final Years

Old Aden like a barrik stove that no-one's lit for years and years – Rudyard Kipling

Aden, the last years; what can be written about them? Perhaps enough to fill a book or two.

Unlike Suez, where I took part in the action and knew nothing about what went on behind the scenes, in Aden I was both an observer of the action at close quarters and a participant in the intrigues and politics behind the scenes.

It takes nearly a book to set the scene but I will try to be brief and reasonably accurate. I propose only to relate some of the highlights that affected me personally during the last two years of British presence in Aden.

After working for the Jamaican Government the War Office could still manage without my services and loaned me to the Colonial Office. There was one advantage, one flew first class.

So in October 1965 I took over from Brigadier Bernard Penfold the post of Security Operations Advisor to the High Commissioner for Aden and the Protectorate of South Arabia. A fine mouthful which almost sums it all up.

Once upon a time the Governor of Aden was solely responsible for the defence and security of Aden and the Protectorate. The pastime of the tough up-country tribesmen was raiding: armed as they were then with old blunderbusses, it was little more dangerous than a rugby match between Welsh or Scottish clans. However, after Suez Nasser took an active part in the Yemen, inciting them against British and, worse still, arming the tribesmen with modern Russian and Czech weapons. Operations and security became a serious business and the then High Commissioner, Sir Kennedy Trevaskis, applied for and got a military adviser to help deal with it. Ken Trevaskis was a chum of mine at Cambridge and he would have liked to have me with him but before this could happen he fell foul of the Labour Government and left.

At the same time Middle East Command set itself up in Aden with a Commander-in-Chief and two-star officers in command of each of the three Services. Naturally these people thought they should be controlling the military operations. Many of the troops were local but British servicemen became increasingly involved, suffering casualties.

By the time I arrived the job of the Security Operations Advisor (SOA) to the High Commissioner (HE) basically was to represent HE's views – which, in turn, had to contain the views of the Foreign Office – to the military commanders. Only too often their views did not exactly coinçide. If all went smoothly nobody was interested in what I had to say. When, not infrequently, it did not I was a convenient whipping boy whom both sides could blame. My main operational function was to process requests for air strikes by the RAF.

Briefly the set-up: at Government House, above and apart from Aden, was HE, Sir Richard Turnbull; at Steamer Point, the opposite side, HQ Middle East Command, C-in-C Admiral Sir Michael Le Fanu; down in Aden the State Government Offices, Deputy High Commissioner, Tom Oates; at Al Ittihad, between Aden and Little Aden, Government offices of the Western Aden Protectorate (WAP), British Agent Robin Young. Finally, not to be forgotten – which it often was – at Mukalla, 300 miles east along the coast, the main city of the Eastern Protectorate (EAP), Resident Adviser Ted Eyre.

I found myself on various top-level comittees at all these places (except Mukalla) and flitted between them in my own car, a white Mini Traveller, driving myself. I lived outside the military protected area in a pleasant Government house in Khormaksar. For most intents and purposes I was a civilian though I did get some help from the Army concerning servants. For over a year I lived as a grass widow and 'did' for myself.

At first the operational situation was reasonably under control apart from the odd incident and I was able to travel all over the Protectorate in comparative safety. I visited the Federal Regular Army (FRA) posts in the Sheikhdoms in WAP mainly by helicopter, and went over the ground in the RADFAN where 3 Para had fought a victorious campaign eighteen months before.

I also went to the fabulous Wadi Hadramut in EAP. This is a lovely fertile valley some 200 miles up in the hinterland from Mukalla. It boasted two towns which, as one approached them in the shimmering heat, for a while resembled the skyline of any American city. On closer inspection the 'skyscrapers' turned out to be moderately tall mud buildings and very disappointing. But the whole area was a prosperous and peaceful oasis amidst the hostile mountains and sands of most of South Arabia.

Early in 1966 my mother, who had been nursing my father, came out for a much-needed break. Sadly, shortly after her arrival he died suddenly in hospital and we had to fly home to arrange the funeral and sort out our affairs. I soon had to return to Aden and she followed a little later.

We had been beginning to make some progress both against Nasser in the Yemen and in persuading the reluctant partners in the South Arabian Federation of Sheikhdoms and Aden State that there was some future in working together towards a stable Government protected by their own troops and capable of taking over from us. It was implied that we could retain a base in neutral Little Aden where both an oil refinery and a splendid new Army cantonment were just being completed.

Then out of the blue in February 1966 came an announcement by the Labour Government that British troops would be withdrawn from Aden by 1968 without any commitment for the defence of the new State after independence. We were unilaterally breaking solemn treaties of protection, having previously chivvied the Sheikhs into sticking to the treaties with us.

Lord Beswick was sent out to break the news in advance. We organised a meeting at Al Ittihad of the Rulers and leaders of the Federal Government. They could hardly believe what Lord Beswick had to tell them and thought perhaps the translation was wrong. But it was not.

These people had been our friends who supported and trusted us. Branded by terrorists as 'lackeys of Britain' they were now being virtually abandoned. Yet they continued to work with us towards some form of stability throughout the rest of the year. Men like the Minister for Security, the stout-hearted Sultan Saleh, and the Foreign Minister, Sheikh Mohammed Farid.

But if this unfortunate announcement by the Government was a tragic shock for our supporters it was a godsend for our enemies. Nasser renewed his flagging activities in the Yemen and the leaders of the terrorist groups redoubled their efforts, resulting in an increase in incidents. At this stage it was not clear which of the terrorist organisations – FLOSY or NLF – would prevail but both were dangerous. The Trades Unions in Aden, who naturally had Labour sympathy, also tried to get in on the act and could cause trouble by calling strikes.

Although terrorism, and violence increased it did not all happen at once. For a time most of the incidents were confined to the Crater district not much visited by Europeans. The British soldier bore the brunt of the trouble and he was magnificent as ever. The Infantry were on unaccompanied tours and successfully protected the families of the rest of us. Brave and wise decisions were made to allow the older children to join their families in the holidays and my daughter Jane flew out three times on the 'Lollipop Special'. Happily none came to any harm during this period. Thanks to the soldiers they could enjoy the lovely beaches and there was plenty of sport for all in Aden.

Cricket was the major summer game as in UK. I was pleased to be Chairman of the Combined Services Cricket Board. There were unit games on hot, sandy grounds culminating in inter-Service matches. We organisd a Combined Services side to tour Kenya and played two matches for trophies against the civilians. The Indian Community in Aden could still raise a very strong side but they could not get much practice as they could only play when we made careful arrangements to let them inside the wire to our grounds.

We kept it going right up to the end and as late as September 1967 I organised a match between we Colonial Administrators called the 'Imperialists' and a team from the many critical newspaper correspondents called the 'Wanderers'. The fame of this contest even reached the United States as this extract from the *New York Times* illustrates:

'The two teams struggled through a searingly hot Arabian afternoon. In the end, Brigadier Crook's "slow spin" (curve ball) pitch helped the Imperialists to prevail.

'The Governor, Sir Humphrey Trevalyan, was in the cheering section but raised his voice only to inquire "Who's that chap there?" when a bearded Tribesman wandered onto the field. It was Brigadier Crook's bodyguard.' (This is part of a cutting from the *New York Times* which was sent to me by my old staff college friend General Bill Yarborough.)

Throughout 1966 we continued to try to create a viable government to whom we could hand over. My part was to help raise and equip effective defence forces at which I worked very hard.

It did at least involve visits back to UK where, based on the Foreign Office actively backed by HE, we endeavoured to prise money, men and machines out of Whitehall for South Arabia.

I dealt with the Ministry of Defence where the Army and the Royal Air Force were reasonably forthcoming. But the Royal Navy were strangely intractable. Not even a word from our C-in-C, Admiral Le Fanu, seemed to make any difference.

I took a delegation from South Arabia to see the Minister of Defence, Mr Healey. I came out from the interview confused and ashamed. Even if you do not

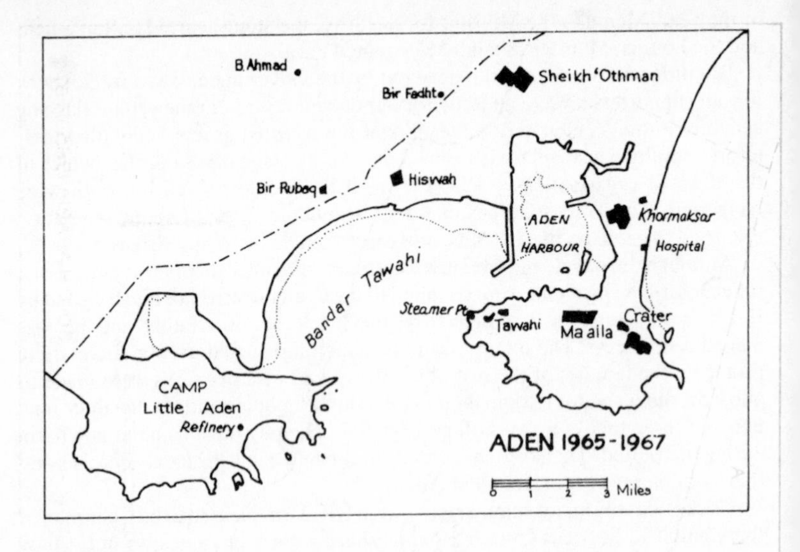

like Sultans and prefer trades union leaders there is no need to let it show.

Back in Aden I was thoroughly involved in a task which interested me very much. I was appointed Chairman of a Board to review the pay of all ranks in the Federal Forces, *ie* the Federal Guard (FG) as well as the FRA. It was later extended to cover the Armed Forces in the EAP. The representative from the Finance Department was a very sensible chap and we managed to get our recommendations accepted. This meant an average pay rise of 25% which gave the soldier some status in South Arabia.

When I went to Mukalla I stayed with Colonel Pat Gray, the Commandant of the Hadramut Bedouin Legion (HBL). This was a lightly armed force of some 1,500 men with a few British offices sponsored by the Colonial Office. It had a wide-ranging role of maintaining security amongst the tribes and manned 'Beau Geste' forts in the desert. Inevitably it had problems.

The Deputy High Commissioner and I went to Mukalla for the inauguration ceremony of a new Sultan of Quaiti, Sultan Chaleb Ben Awadh. He was a young man of eighteen recently returned from being educated in England. It was an interesting affair with much feasting and fireworks.

I was deeply shocked when one morning I heard that Pat Gray had been shot and killed by his Arab orderly and his wife Edith seriously wounded. I obtained a Beaver aircraft and dashed over to find out what was happening. There was no sign of mutiny among the HBL, only sorrow, and I was able to stabilise the situation. We persuaded the Military Adviser to the Resident, the experienced Colonel Eric Johnson, to take over the HBL. Happily, Mrs Gray recovered after a long spell in hospital.

It transpired that the shooting was just an isolated act of craziness by Pat's 'faithful' orderly. But it brought to the forefront just how dicey was the position of a British officer serving with Arabs and it became more precarious for those in the Federal Forces as the situation worsened. People whom I knew well like Colonel 'Blick' Waring of the Queen's Own stationed up country with the FRA and

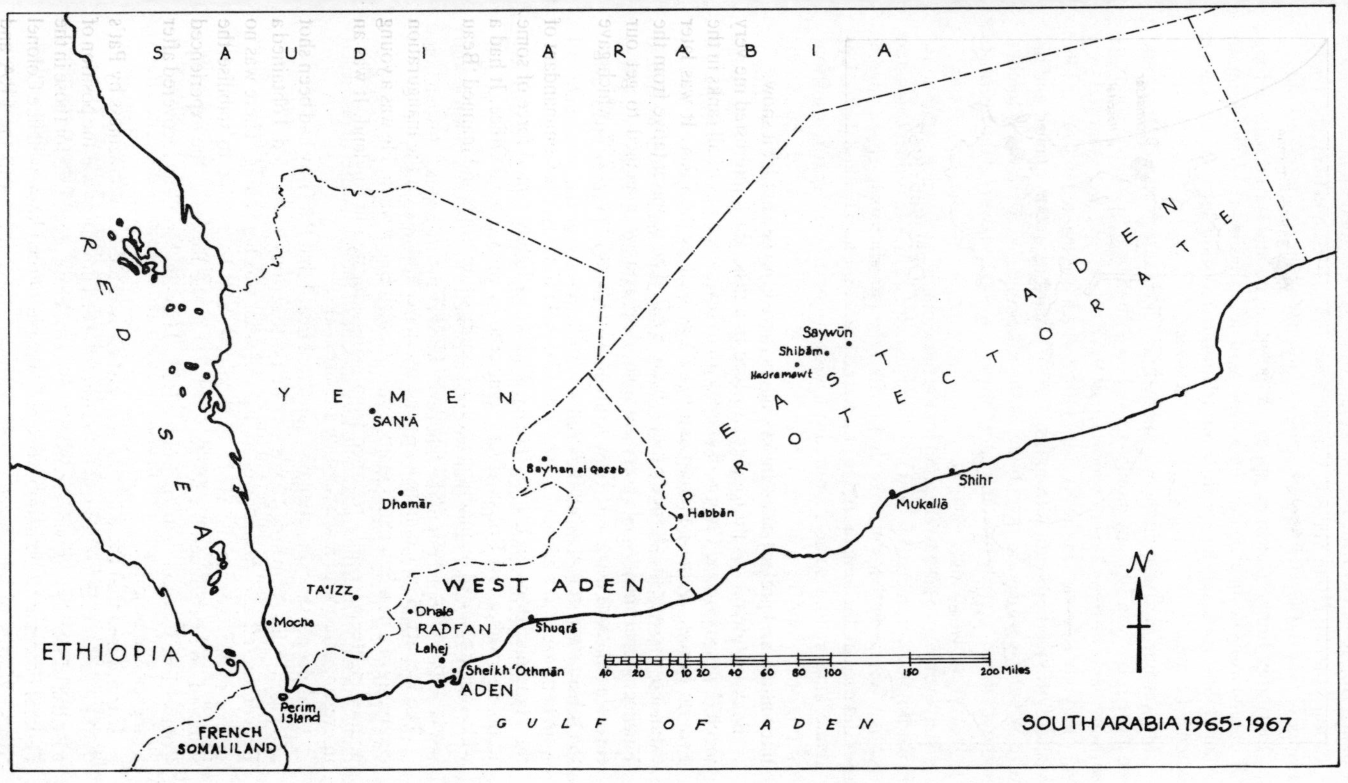

SAUDI ARABIA
EASTERN ADEN PROTECTORATE
Saywūn
Shibām
Hadramawt
YEMEN
SAN'Ā
Bayhan al Qasab
Dhamār
Habbān
Shihr
Mukallā
N
RED SEA
TA'IZZ
WEST ADEN
Mocha
Dhala
RADFAN
Shuqrā
ETHIOPIA
Lahej
Sheikh 'Othmān
ADEN
40 20 0 10 20 40 60 80 100 150 200 Miles
Perim Island
FRENCH SOMALILAND
GULF OF ADEN
SOUTH ARABIA 1965-1967

Colonel Bill Bowen with the FG. And there were my very good friends Brigadiers Gordon Viner and John Mallard, Commanders of the FRA and FG respectively. Happily, they did survive unscathed but, sadly, not all the junior officers did.

Inevitably Jumbo Courtney appeared on the scene and stayed with us for a short time while he investigated the prospects of doing business with merchants in Aden. Not surprisingly he saw little future for this and soon departed for Kuwait whence he came.

My wartime marriage, in the way these things did, came to mean nothing and we parted. Early in 1967 my mother set sail on a small boat to Aden in company with my fiancée, Betty Lown, widow of an RAF officer. We were married by a very nervous Registrar in the Registry Office which was located in Crater. John Mallard provided protection from his Federal Guard as well as himself and his wife Wendy as witnesses; my mother as the other one. We were safely hitched without a hitch but only two days later the place was taken over by the terrorists and no one could go there again.

That evening we gave a reception for the flora and fauna of Aden at our house in Khormaksar protected by 1 Para who had just arrived in Aden under command of Mike Walsh. Perhaps mistakenly I invited the parachutists to check anyone they did not like the look of. Being new to the place they hardly liked the look of anyone and treated some of our distinguished guests with grave suspicion, insisting on frisking them and demanding proof of identity. It caused a bit of a stir but it was evidence of just how efficient the paras were going to be.

One day it rained, really rained in a tropical downpour: and it did the same throughout the next day. This occurred once every seven years apparently. Of course there were no proper drains and there was flooding everywhere. We had no water or electricity and decided to go into Aden for a meal. First we had to acquire a landrover which stuck in the mud in an isolated spot. Betty and I were trying to extricate it when a party of Arab males appeared. Frankly I was rather apprehensive but to be fair all they did was to help push us out with smiles all round.

We then proceeded into Aden with both my mother and Jane on board. We stopped outside the Crescent Hotel where there was obviously some muddy water around, but rather more than we had bargained for. When my mother, who is not very tall, stepped out of the landrover we very nearly lost her down a hole and the water came up to her neck! But we dried her out and got a meal.

As a result, for a few days there was actually some green vegetation to be seen around Aden on which the goats could feed instead of their usual diet of discarded cigarette packets.

My mother bought us a sailing dinghy – *Ticopia* – to give us some safe recreation away from the dangers of the land. Originally she was berthed down at Steamer Point where we took her out without knowing much about her. We soon arrived at the beginning of the Indian Ocean where I capsized her in shark waters trying to go about. Shouting to Betty to swim and rescue the bailer I managed to right her. However, I succeeded in doing it again and once more deposited Betty into the ocean. This was too much for the watchers at the RAF Yacht Club ashore who dashed out and gallantly rescued Betty leaving me to my own devices.

We discovered that the temperamental *Ticopia* needed a couple of rocks in her bow to make her respond normally. Having discovered this, we had no more trouble and sailed her up the harbour past Ma'alla to a berth near home opposite

Slave Island. We enjoyed some pleasant sailing in the calmer, if murky, waters there.

Eventually *Ticopia* fetched up at a berth in Lyme Regis, Dorset, thanks to airborne initiative which needs no explanation.

To return to the troublesome situation in South Arabia which was steadily getting worse. Acts of terrorism, strikes and riots became more common. As if this was not enough we were burdened with a plague of visiting missions.

The first was from Amnesty International at our request. Without checking the facts they had accused us of ill-treating internees. They were in fact among the better-off people in Aden as was shown when they were let out. Their representative was an extraordinary person who barely saw the internees, was terrified throughout, and left as soon as he could without achieving anything.

It was suggested that perhaps the United Nations could help in the search for a stable government to whom we could hand over. Accordingly, a delegation from the prejudiced Committee on Colonialism consisting of a representative from Mali, Afghanistan and Venezuela was sent. On their way to Aden they spent some time in Cairo with Nasser and the terrorist leaders. This allowed time for our terrorists to prepare a campaign of violence to prove how awful was the repression by the British.

The Seaview Hotel on Khormaksar beach was turned into a fortress to house them in safety. It was not far from Crater, centre of the unrest, where the mobs reacted noisily and violently. Sir Richard Turnbull politely flew by helicopter to greet them there to save them going to Government House and everything was done to make them secure and comfortable.

Their behaviour was incredible, an utter farce which would have been laughable if it had not been so tragic. They refused to deal with any members of the Federal Government and the prisoners refused to deal with them. Most of the time they stayed inside their hotel fortified by a case of HE's best champagne. Certainly there was a great deal of unpleasantness all around. The Arabs took the opportunity to fight amongst themselves as well as attacking us and much ammunition was expended. The Northumberland Fusiliers acquitted themselves admirably under much provocation and danger; eight were wounded.

The delegation made no attempt to assess the situation and complained childishly about everything. They cut short their visit and left hurriedly amidst squabbles about having their baggage searched before being allowed on the plane.

Sir Richard Turnbull's handling of this sorry business was, as ever, courteous, calm and sensible, yet he was apparently blamed for the fiasco though it was none of his making. He returned to UK to discuss it with the Foreign Secretary, George Brown, and to his surprise and our horror was peremptorily sacked by him on the spot. He was a devoted, loyal and very efficient servant of his country and has been very shabbily treated.

The outcome was yet another mission, this one of our own making, led by Lord Shackleton. They came out apparently imagining that they could sort out the whole mess. In practice they achieved nothing except to make a thorough nuisance of themselves. They were given accommodation in the Government House compound and left it in a disgusting state like a gang of hooligans.

The Government brought the distinguished diplomat, Sir Humphrey Trevelyan, out of retirement to replace Sir Richard with a different brief and approach.

Soon after his arrival we went up to Beihan to call on the Sultan. We were shown the place in the desert where the Queen of Sheba was supposed to have met King Solomon and then attended a 'fadhl' or feast with the Sultan. Afterwards we were standing on the flat roof of the guesthouse in bright moonlight when I remarked to HE:

'The trouble with these people is that they don't play cricket.'

'What do you mean?' HE enquired.

'Most other races with whom we have had dealings do play cricket and it seems to help us to get on with each other better,' I replied.

'Well I don't play cricket!'

Arabs do not usually make war on women but sometimes they find themselves in the way. A tragic example of this occurred at a party attended by security and intelligence officers and their wives and secretaries. As often happened at parties in Arabia the ladies gossiped at one end of the room and the men talked shop at the other. In this instance a bomb had been planted in a bookcase to get the security men but, alas, it went off at the ladies' end of the room, killing two and wounding seven; no men were hurt.

Apart from the horror of this tragedy it left the Secretariat short of security-cleared staff. Betty was asked to do a shift on the High Commissioner's telephone exchange at Government House. She used to be driven there in a military vehicle with an armed escort while I still went there through Ma'alla in my Mini.

On 1 June 1967 we were invited to attend a ceremonial parade to mark the amalgamation of the Federal Regular Army and the Federal Guard into one force to be designated the South Arabian Army on 'Armed Forces Day'.

Betty put on her best dress and wedding hat and on the way we went past the road which went to Sheik Otman, a tough township controlled by 1 Para. At the checkpoint we found Mike Walsh dressed in contrast for battle in combat kit and heard firing down the road. Mike was pleased to see us and delighted by Betty's hat which he said made his day.

We left him to his war and went on to the parade ground which was an empty piece of sand away from everywhere. The parade was attended by everyone of note, including HE, the C-in-C and Federal Ministers. They all sat in the front row during endless speeches under the guns of Scout cars and 25-pounders pointing straight at us. One could not help wondering whether some of the Arabian soldiery might be tempted to stage a coup by wiping out the 'Establishment' in one fell swoop. It would have been so easy but nothing of the kind occurred.

But it would not have been possible to stage such a parade a month later.

We planned to get away from the heat and horrors of Aden by going for a break in the hills of Somalia at Hargeysa. We were about to embark on an Aden Airways plane and our luggage was already on board when a tremendous hubbub broke out in the airport. I discovered that Nasser had attacked Israel and the Six Day War had started. I managed to retrieve our baggage and we returned to the house to the surprise and dismay of the servants.

We know now that Nasser lost this war but there were to be unexpected ramifications for us. Cairo radio poured out lies that British and American air forces had intervened, causing their defeat. It was not immediately appreciated what effect this propaganda would have on some of the soldiers in the South Arabian Armed Forces.

Rumours proliferated amongst them about the behaviour of British troops and on 20 June two terrible events took place.

First a truck full of men of the Royal Corps of Transport returning to their barracks from the range was fired on by disgruntled Arab soldiers in neighbouring Champion Lines and eight were killed. This took place not far from some British married quarters and order had to be restored quickly by British troops. This was done effectively but led to rumours that British soldiers were attacking the Arab army.

Next, routine patrols of the Northumberland Fusiliers who were accompanied by advance parties from the Argyll and Sutherland Highlanders were fired on unexpectedly by the Armed Police as they drove through a pass which led from Aden to Crater. Considerable confused fighting ensued and at least ten British soldiers were killed and some missing. Mobs took over Crater rioting, looting and killing. The troops on the spot were understandably furious that they were not allowed to go in and avenge their dead comrades.

But it was not as straightforward as that. The situation of other Britons had to be taken into account. While this was going on I myself, for instance, was in my office at Al Ittihad along with some other British personnel including females. They were even a few families in married quarters out there. There were no British troops at all and we were guarded by the Federal Guard. As some of them had just mutinied in Aden there was no knowing what these would do.

In fact they took little interest in us and I immediately organised a convoy of the ladies which got safely to Aden. We all had to evacuate the Federal Government buildings at Ittihad.

Time had to be gained for this and other similar operations amidst the inflammatory situation at Crater. The soldiers there, particularly the newly arrived Argylls, did not know this or realise that precipitate action by them might be jeopardising the lives of others elsewhere. Certainly they put mine in jeopardy.

Sheik Otman was located just outside Aden at the beginning of the Dhala road. The situation there was in some respects similar to Crater. It was efficiently taken care of by 1 Para. A visit to them was an exciting and exhilarating business. It was great to be amongst one's own kind again and I had many friends in the Messes: the RSM, Brian Sharman, was one of my sergeants in 3 Para.

Mike Walsh had established a strongpoint from which to dominate the place which soon became known as 'Fort Walsh' by the Press, which started to give him a lot of publicity which he welcomed on behalf of his soldiers rather than himself, especially as the Argylls in Crater were getting even more. I understood his motives but took the liberty of reminding him that publicity at Suez had never done me any good and that he would be well advised to play it down. Wisely he did so and 1 Para did a first-class job without fuss. Meanwhile Lieutenant-Colonel Mitchell commanding the Argylls actively sought publicity for his men. The result: Mike Walsh was awarded a DSO whilst Mitchell received a Mention in Despatches.

A word about 'Mad Mitch' whom I met but did not know well. He was clearly an extremely efficient, dedicated officer. Impulsive, he required good handling; given it he would have been brilliant, but he did not get it and subsequently was shabbily treated.

I now had an office in Government House but just before I left Ittihad Captain Heaney, who also worked there and drove a white Mini like mine, was ambushed and killed on the road to it. I acquired a landrover but the driver and vehicle were abducted and never seen again. I began to wonder if someone out there didn't like me.

As I have said, we lived in a house outside the wire near the airfield at Khormaksar. I had been in the habit of walking the dog round the neighbourhood past the well-guarded house of Hussein Ali Bayoumi, an Adeni businessman who for a short while was Prime Minister designate at the new Federal Government. But he failed to form a cabinet and resigned. This made our area more insalubrious. On two nights there was shooting round our house. The dog was a jolly local breed who came with the house. Then he deserted us and insisted on remaining in safety behind the wire at RAF Khormaksar. The cook, Mahoub, suddenly took off for the Yemen without even waiting for his pay! It seemed it must be time for us to leave too.

After some difficulty we were fortunate enough to obtain a very nice apartment in a block of flats at Steamer Point whose occupant had fled. It was situated high up, right on the coast looking out to sea, and from the balcony it was like being on the bridge of a ship. Close behind us towered the rocky heights of Sham Shan mountain which I did not climb before breakfast! Dawns were spectacular. It was a good place in which to end our time in Aden and also to entertain battle-weary Para officers.

We could reach Government House in safety and so missed the very unpleasant conditions which were happening outside. By now all the families had been evacuated. Betty remained at her post at HE's telephone exchange and was once mortared there: no one was hurt. There were other ladies still working in government offices but Betty became the last Service wife left in Aden.

Although there was plenty for her to do, it became apparent that there was no longer a job for a Security Operations Advisor. So we were allowed to leave a month before the end. It was to be a beastly, bloody month in which the NLF prevailed and we were lucky to miss it.

1 Para had left Sheik Otman with resulting death and destruction and taken up positions in the shortened perimeter along the saltpans guarding the runway of Khormaksar airfield. It was a very necessary task which proved dull and very uncomfortable. We were not there to see them march down the runway smartly dressed as on a ceremonial parade on the day before the final evacuation.

On the day we left Mike provided an armoured vehicle to pick us up at dawn from Steamer Point and take us to Khormaksar airfield past Ma'alla through which I had motored so many times. It was now no place to be. Mike himself saw us off with some relief. So my strange, varied and hectic tour in South Arabia ended at least in a military fashion and some style.

25

Marking Time

They also serve who only stand and wait – John Milton

The Royal Naval College, Greenwich, consists of a splendid collection of historic buildings beside the River Thames. A Palace was built there early in the fifteenth century where Queen Elizabeth I was born. The College was originally designed by Christopher Wren as a Naval Hospital and subsequently other distinguished architects were concerned in its development. It became a College in 1873. Perhaps the most prestigious building is the Painted Hall with its decorations by Sir James Thornhill, including on the ceiling 173½ bosoms (half of one bosom is covered). It is still used for Royal and State occasions but, happily, it is also the Officers' Mess where we wined and dined in style.

It was to this establishment that I was fortunate enough to be sent on a Senior Officers' War Course for six months which was to prove very good value.

Before going to the course there was a sting in the tail from Aden. The car I had there was in good shape and in spite of frequent strikes by dockers we managed to get it loaded on a ship to UK. But she arrived at a time when there was a strike and no one would unload her. So the poor little car hung around on deck for eight weeks in the winter before eventually being offloaded at Harwich, by now considerably the worse for wear. Ironically the British docker had succeeded in doing what his Adeni counterpart had not.

We were allocated a quarter in a Territorial Army building in the middle of the heath of Blackheath. It was almost rural amidst south-east London and safe for a dog. The stone entrance and staircase were not pretty, reminiscent of 'the buildings', but the flat on the top floor was not at all bad and we could see the spires of seven London churches from the balcony. At a nearby pub, the *Green Man* now demolished, there were some splendid jazz sessions.

The course itself was well run under the direction of Captain Alan Smalley. One of my fellow students was Captain Darby George whom I had known when in command of *HMS Londonderry* in the West Indies and later as Chief of Staff to the Admiral in Aden. Sadly, the Admiral President, Admiral Sir Horace Lydden, died very suddenly early on in the course which was a great shock and loss.

The syllabus was a judicious mixture of carrot and stick. There was an excellent programme of visits to the most interesting establishments in all three Services. We went to sea at both Portsmouth and Londonderry and went aboard a nuclear submarine at Faslane. We visited Royal Air Force Stations in Lincolnshire which was to lead to interesting developments in my retirement. We also had a spell at Cambridge University where I was hospitably entertained at my old College, Emmanuel. Another interesting visit was to the Headquarters of NATO outside Brussels, enabling us to do a tour of the battlefield at Waterloo which was fascinating. Last but not least we went to Berlin where we crossed the Wall to East Berlin and I distinguished (or disgraced) myself by rendering some good old jazz numbers in a Berlin night club in fine style to distinct applause. But unlike the old days at Hatchetts where I was rewarded for my efforts, in Berlin when I came to leave I was presented with a bill for the band.

We worked hard at some paper exercises and had some very distinguished persons to talk to us, including Minister of Defence Healey and writer Chapman Pincher. One impressed me; one did not.

Altogether the SOWC at Greenwich proved a very worthwhile and illuminating episode in my army life.

After Greenwich I was posted to command Rhine Area in Germany but there was an eight months' period before I was required to take over. I was offered a choice between 'gardening leave' and a 'funny' job. I chose the latter.

As my name is not Peter Wright I do not propose to relate in detail the nature of my work for the 'funnies'. Suffice to say that it entailed being based in Kampala, Uganda and included seven safari trips through Game Parks in East Africa and a voyage, complete with car, round Lake Victoria, all at Her Majesty's expense.

We found the people in Uganda charming and a walk through the streets of Kampala at night was a great deal safer than it would have been in some districts of London at that time. I met the abominable Idi Amin, then Head of the Army. He had as his chief military adviser a much-decorated Israeli Parachutist Brigadier. No wonder the subsequent raid on Entebbe was such a success!

The game parks were well stocked at this time and we were able to take good photos of all sorts of animals, including lions, tigers, elephants and crocodiles. They were usually indifferent to our presence but we did encounter an angry rhino and Betty was convinced that the nearby trumpeting elephant was suffering from toothache which does not improve their normally placid temper.

We were always on our own and so there were some interesting moments. We developed a puncture in lion country where you are not supposed to get out of the car. I am not normally very expert in changing a wheel but I managed this one in record time. On another occasion we were caught in a sudden downpour towards evening. What had been a hard, sandy track rapidly turned into a soft, muddy one. We had a hair-raising drive back to base, slithering, sliding and sometimes almost sticking. But our sturdy Ford Corsair made it. On the other hand, she broke down in the oddest of places and we once spent hours in a remote African village while the 'mechanic' carried out some Heath Robinson repairs which worked well enough to allow us to stagger home.

After six months our time in Africa came to an end. It certainly had not been wasted but had been an unusual, interesting and at times exciting experience.

We flew home first class via Athens where we spent a very pleasant week.

26

Finale

All work and no play makes Tom a dull boy – Proverb

For my final assignment I was appointed to command Rhine Area. This comprised all the units in the British Army of the Rhine (BAOR) behind the river Rhine from our Headquarters at Dusseldorf on the river to a Base at Antwerp in Belgium. We were responsible for the administration of literally hundreds of big and small units and detachments. There were ten large garrisons including Rheindahlen Garrison which contained the headquarters of both BAOR and Northern Army Group (NORTHAG). It was estimated that in some way or other I was responsible for some 30,000 souls divided, like Gaul, into three parts, 10,000 soldiers; 10,000 uniformed foreign workers ('Green Men'); and 10,000 civilians, families and dependants.

This responsibility was very slight in many cases. Nevertheless anyone connected with the Army in Germany came within the Army's jurisdiction for legal matters. Under an agreement the German authorities referred serious civil cases to us for action. This applied to everyone from the C-in-C's wife onwards.

Serious cases could only be dealt with by Courts Martial. This could cause misunderstandings. For example, a young girl of eighteen working for exams killed a German civilian in a car accident. She was undoubtedly negligent but the case was handed over to us by the German authorities. It was so serious that it had to be dealt with by a Court Martial. This caused an outcry in some sections of the British Press with headlines about the bullying by Blimpish Army Officers of an innocent young girl, jeopardising her career, etc. In fact she was treated very kindly and only fined. Had she remained under German civil jurisdiction she would almost certainly have been given a term of imprisonment.

Such civilian cases were fortunately rare but amongst the soldiery inevitably there were only too many offences committed leading to a Court Martial. The legal system has subsequently been changed but at that time all courts martial were referred to the Area Commander for confirmation or otherwise. Obviously all the proceedings had to be legally correct or I was in trouble. Happily I was blessed with a wonderful Retired Officer, Ben Lyon, who dealt with everything legal immaculately and had all the right answers. He had immediate, direct access to me at all times and life could have been a misery without him.

One was much involved with people and their personal problems, including such persons as schoolmasters and the NAAFI Manager in addition to officers and soldiers. Confidential Reports were a major headache. I was the 'superior reporting officer' for all majors and above and there were an awful lot of them, some tucked away in strange places. One could not possibly get to know them all but in too many cases had to rely on one's knowledge of the initiating officer. As it might affect an officer's career I can in all honesty say that I did my best to be helpful and fair.

But enough of this rather heavy stuff. Life for me in Rhine Area was fun and I did my best to make it so for others. Soldiering should be fun.

The main units in the Area with the exception of Signals were administrative, hospitals, ordnance depots, workshops and the like. The soldiers were specialists and had to be proficient in their specialist role. But they also had to be soldiers capable of fighting. My task and aim was to see that sufficient training was done to ensure that all ranks could at the drop of a hat lay aside their individual specialities and play their part as a fighting soldier. To this end I encouraged them to get away from their desks and benches and carry out some meaningful training and at the same time have some fun.

We were fortunate enough to live in an excellent quarter, a large house which had been a Guards Officers' Mess. It had a lovely dining-room which could seat eighteen and often did. It was far superior to any of the generals' quarters in Rheindahlen which did not please some of them when they came to dine. It was situated in a superior suburb outside Dusseldorf called Gerresheim: all around were smart houses of prosperous Germans. But one was reminded sharply of what it had all been about by coming across, a short walk away, a gloomy grove which contained a memorial and the mass grave of a large number of Russian prisoners of war who had been murdered and buried there.

Mention of Russians reminds one of a curious and tiresome episode.

A short distance from us was a cul-de-sac containing some decent houses in one of which lived my Deputy, David Gilchrist and his wife Rosemary. The area was discreet and secure and could be sealed off.

Now at this time there was in BAOR a Russian Military Mission whose members under strict supervision were allowed to see a little of what went on in the British Zone. They had to live somewhere and the powers-that-be decided to move them to this area in Gerresheim. Preparations were put in hand to render the buildings suitable for occupation by Russians. Naturally the Gilchrists were very upset at the prospect of having to move from their nice quarter to a noisy one on the edge of the airfield. The whole business was conducted in great secrecy but I was able to allow the Gilchrists to remain until the last minute. So they stuck it out while certain structural alterations were carried out around them. In the end their perseverance was rewarded as the Russians never came but I hate to think what it did to their private life.

We had to do a lot of entertaining and it was a big establishment for Betty to run but we were allowed an adequate staff. There were several civilian ladies including a cook/housekeeper, and I had a much needed live-in batman. First I inherited Lance-Bombadier Collins who came from the Royal Malta Artillery. When the Regiment left BAOR to return to Malta he went with them. He was a splendid chap and I am sure must now be a major domo in some establishment in Malta. He was succeeded by another very good fellow, Lance-Corporal Bishop, kindly provided by my parent Regiment, the Queen's Own, serving in 1 Corps.

There was also a gardener, a 'Green Man' from the Labour Force. He could be satisfactory and was certainly a success as Father Christmas at the children's party. But, like many 'Green Men', he suffered from bouts of depression and had a drink problem. When I could not provide him with a new lawnmower he took agin' me and one day got hold of my brief case and flung it into the woods behind us. Fortunately it was found after a search. But, worse still, while washing up at a dinner party he managed to insert some soap into the cooking pans. It was soon discovered by the cook but Betty never knew whether any of the guests politely suffered in silence.

Then there was the driver from the Royal Corps of Transport, Corporal Keenagh. He was a brilliant driver and steered us safely and swiftly through all sorts of places, cities and countries. We had to rely on him to take us to the right place and very occasionally he had a mental blackout and took us to the wrong one. The first and worst such an occasion was when shortly after my arrival he and I drove to meet Betty who was bringing our new Ford Capri across from England. I arranged to meet her at a roundabout on the road from Ostend just outside Brussels which Corporal Keenagh confidently said he knew. We had to start at dawn and he arrived late. We drove at speed the 120 miles to this roundabout to find nobody there. I waited some time with growing anxiety making fruitless enquiries of passing British motorists. Eventually, with considerable misgiving I abandoned the rendezvous and went in search of her. Happily we soon found her at the right roundabout further down the motorway where she had been correctly waiting with equal growing anxiety. Nevertheless Keenagh was a very likeable man, an agreeable travelling companion, and we became very fond of him.

My own pet loves were well catered for in Rhine Area.

First, cricket; I was very pleased to be asked to be Chairman of the BAOR Cricket Association. We had an excellent fixture list including matches against the MCC, the Danes and the Dutch. We built up a very good BAOR side under the admirable captaincy of Major Noel McDonnell. Amongst a number of good players there was an absolutely outstanding one, Sergeant H.O. Bradshaw, REME, who topped both the bowling and batting averages and would have been an asset to a good West Indian side. We did not lose a match and beat the Danes in Denmark – quite a feat – and the RAF for the first time in six years. There was plenty of unit cricket and we ran a decent team at HQ Rhine Area. Padre Jerry Murphy and I sometimes opened the innings and I was not out in my last innings in the Army.

Next, jazz; there was a flourishing Dramatic and Music Association in Dusseldorf including an enthusiastic jazz club. We played records and ended with a 'Jam' session at which Father 'Fingers' Hartley was the leading light on the piano. Before leaving I presented the Club with a tape of my very favourite records including one of myself 'with vocal refrain'.

As I have said, Rheindahlen contained the large staffs of both BAOR and NORTHAG including a number of senior and allied officers. The unfortunate Garrison Commander had to be a very brave and thick-skinned officer. The job required the qualities of a holder of the Victoria Cross and there was one in the shape of Colonel Pat Porteous, VC. When he had had enough his place was taken by an equally stout-hearted officer, Colonel Charles Boynton. They suffered from being the recipients of numerous mainly petty complaints such as the length of the grass outside an office. I briefed them to reply politely saying: 'Yes, sir, I will do my best, but will you please take up the matter with my Commander in Dusseldorf?' Fortunately they rarely did.

On the other hand, the Garrison Commander Antwerp had a comparatively pleasant job. He was in charge of the supply and ordnance establishments of the Advanced Base at Emblem just outside Antwerp. It was admirably run by Col Tony des Harper who had come straight there from being our military man in Moscow and so was well suited to doing the same and showing the flag in Belgium.

For instance, he held a parade to celebrate Her Majesty the Queen's Official Birthday which was attended by the British Ambassador as well as many Belgian dignitaries. I enjoyed my visits there and took the opportunity of once again touring the battlefield at Waterloo and marvelling at the wonderful military skill, courage and leadership of Wellington.

We had many visitors, among the most memorable being Mr Hattersley, the Bishop of Leicester and the Quarter Master General, General Sir John Read, who distinguished himself by going off in the morning with my scruffy Brigadier's hat instead of his own.

Her Royal Highness The Princess Anne paid a visit to Dusseldorf to lay a foundation stone of the Florence Nightingale Hospital – Florence Nightingale spent a crucial period at the Kaiserworth Hospital near Dusseldorf in 1850 where the experience she gained as a nurse formed the foundation of all her future action and career.

HRH was met by HM Ambassador, Sir Roger Jackling, and various German dignitaries. We met her at the site of the stone-laying ceremony and took the liberty of reminding her of her schooldays at Benenden where my aunt, Miss Beaumont, was one of her teachers. She seemed to recall her with pleasure and to be highly amused.

The Diplomatic people were very pleasant. They hosted us at Bonn when we went for a briefing and in the evening the Ambassador and Lady Jackling gave a splendid party. In the same way the Consul-General at Dusseldorf, Gerald Simpson, and his wife Peggy were very charming and hospitable.

I had to attend a number of German Civic Functions which were always a bit of a strain as my knowledge of German is nil. Occasionally I made a short prepared speech in German without understanding a word.

At one of these I was opening an Anglo/German Road Safety Week and urging my listeners to be particularly careful of the trams which swept swiftly and silently down the middle of the road when there was a loud crash outside. One of them had hit a British car. I was driven to continue in English that they ought to abolish the beastly things altogether. All this was given prominence in the German press.

I was invited to a reception given to welcome a new Commander of the German Army Northern Area and found myself the sole British Army Officer in a room packed with German Army officers. The only person who could speak English assured me that they had all fought on the Russian front! The new arrival was a Major-General Siebl who was a pleasant person with adequate English and we became quite good friends.

The last remaining Railway Unit was stationed in the Area. They were very accommodating people and let me drive a steam engine, thereby fulfilling every schoolboy's dream. They were pleased when I took the C-in-C's train out on an exercise and made good use of it as an officers' mess.

One of the highlights of the Rhine Area year was the Nijmegen Marches. We acted as hosts to all the Service teams taking part and organised a camp in which to feed and accommodate them. A total of over 1,000 marched including 100 females: the RAF produced nearly 400 and around 480 came over from UK. There were two Army Bands and two Pipe Bands from the RAF.

The night before the marches we gave a big Cocktail Party to which we invited officers from everyone taking part, including Allies as well as leading Dutch personalities.

The Dutch themselves were most courteous and hospitable, providing us with excellent seats and motor-cycle outriders to ensure our smooth passage to them and to a reception they gave afterwards. One spent quite a long time in one's seat watching and applauding the thousands of folk marching past the finish.

All this required a deal of organisation which was efficiently done by two Retired Officers, Majors Thorpe and Hawtin. Our part was to look after the VIPs and their wives who came to watch.

Alas, our time in Rhine Area came to a close only too quickly, packed as it was with non-stop activities, official, military, sporting and social. I handed over to Brigadier Geoffrey Bavin RCT and no doubt some people heaved a sigh of relief anticipating the return to a more peaceful way of life.

I made my farewell to the excellent HQ Staff who now included my very dear friend Kip Keenlyside; I am happy to say that I had obtained him a Retired Officer's job just before leaving. Then we had a good send-off from the VIP Lounge at the airport and left in some style. The next day we went down to Dover to meet the faithful Corporal Keenagh who had brought over our car.

An officer is normally given a resettlement course before final retirement. If I could have sent Betty on the 'bricks and mortar course' with the generals at Aldershot it would have been the best value as she is the practical one who can keep the home from falling down. However, this could not be and I had to settle for a Management Appreciation Course at the School of Management Studies sponsored by the Central London Polytechnic. General Sir Charles Harrington was one of my fellow students.

The course was fairly constructive and informative but they tried to turn one into a high-powered salesman which is not really my cup of tea. However, I completed the course and got a nice certificate at the end of it.

Now came the time for my final retirement from active service and to go onto the Reserve, which took effect as I was approaching my 56th birthday; technically nearly a year late. Not that I minded. I would have stayed in the Army *ad infinitum* if wanted.

Post Script

And so I sing my evenin' song – Rudyard Kipling

During my look at civilian employment I decided to continue to try to give service, this time to the Police. The Chief Constable of the Lincolnshire Constabulary appointed me his Force Welfare Officer. I was one of the early holders of such a post and helped pioneer a new concept of welfare for serving and retired police officers and their dependants, both in my own county and throughout the country. Captains RN (retired) Dalgliesh and Little were my counterparts in the Metropolitan Police, and in Devon and Cornwall Lieutenant-Colonel John Chanter who had been on the course with me at Greenwich.

The Royal Navy at Greenwich had sent this Army Officer to see the Royal Air Force in Lincolnshire and Betty had served as a WAAF Officer in the area during the war. Thus we both knew what a pleasant place Lincolnshire really is, very different from some people's ignorant misconceptions. It is not just that 'flat place on the right as you go north' nor is it all dykes and ditches. Parts are attractive, rolling countryside like the Shires, while the Wolds are similar to the South Downs without the people: and the people are welcoming, kind and friendly.

So we were both prepared to treat and enjoy Lincolnshire as 'just another posting'. But we stayed, and only moved once.

First we lived in an old Methodist chapel which Betty skilfully changed into a house (we did not 'convert' it, it 'converted' us). It was a very pleasant, friendly home but in the wrong place, to the north of Lincoln. We kept looking in the south and one Boxing Day drove past a village where a cricket match was being played on an excellent ground. 'That must be a good place to live,' I remarked.

And it came to pass that we did.

We acquired a lovely old property in the small village of Frieston adjoining Caythorpe. Caythorpe not only possessed that cricket ground and a good side to go with it, but on entering the church we discovered that it had an Arnhem Aisle.

Caythorpe had been the wartime home of 1st Airborne Divisional Signal Regiment. It included the White House to which Tony Deane Drummond returned after his adventures at Arnhem.

Nowadays all airborne signallers hold an annual Reunion at Caythorpe during which they go to church, the pubs, and to us for a Garden Party.

Lincolnshire is not only the home of the RAF but also of many wartime units of 1 Airborne Division. Among them my old Battalion, 3 Para, was stationed at Spalding, and 2 Para at Stoke Rochford just south of Grantham where Johnny Frost comes for their Reunion. From our house can be seen Barkston Heath whence the planes and gliders of 9th US Air Force Troop Carrier Command took off for Arnhem.

As might be expected, there are flourishing Branches of the Parachute Regimental Association in the County. One is at Grimsby of which I am a member, one at Spalding of which I have been President, and the latest at Lincoln founded by Lieutenant-Colonel Brian Feehily and the Ron Ward family of which I am its first President.

But as well as veteran parachute soldiers in Lincolnshire there are some young active ones. To my great delight I had the distinction of being appointed Honorary Colonel of 16 (Lincoln) Independent Company, The Parachute Regiment, Territorial Army.

The Company, based on Newport Drill Hall, Lincoln, had the role of acting as the Pathfinder and Patrol Company of 44 Parachute Brigade, TA, and became very proficient at it, beating Regular British and US Army units in patrol competitions.

Sadly, 44 TA Para Brigade was disbanded as such by a Labour Government and no role remained for an independent company. 16 Lincoln Company had shown itself to be too efficient to meet a similar fate and it became part of 15th (Scottish Volunteer) Battalion, The Parachute Regiment. This was pretty satisfactory as they were so far away that we remained in many respects independent. This did not always suit the Commanding Officer, first Pat Wood followed by Edward Gardener. But they were always very civil to us and we were known as their 'English Company'.

We took part in the Parade at Edinburgh when the Colonel-in-Chief of The Regiment, His Royal Highness the Prince of Wales presented new Colours to the Battalion. It was a wonderful occasion blessed with fine if windy weather. The Lincoln Company acquitted themselves very well and in my biased opinion were the best sub-unit on parade. We were also present a year later when the old Colours were laid up in Glasgow Cathedral.

It had to be admitted that it was rather a nonsense for an NCO to travel all the way from Lincoln to Glasgow for a conference with the Regimental Sergeant Major. When it was found that 15 Para could raise an extra company in Scotland it was decided to add the Lincoln Company to the 4th (Volunteer) Battalion, The Parachute Regiment. It was a pity but made economic sense.

4 Para is a very large Territorial Battalion spanning the North and Midlands and was very ably commanded by Hamish McGregor. He did not at first take kindly to some of our independent ways but we managed to win him over, not least by sweeping the board at the first Battalion Rifle Meeting in which we took part.

Throughout this I had the honour of remaining Honorary Colonel of 16 Lincoln Company and of being appointed Deputy Honorary Colonel of 15 (Scottish) Para and later 4 Para. In my time, 16 Company had some excellent Company Commanders starting with Huw Pike, but there were periods when the Company was without a Regular officer. My office at County Police Headquarters was just down the road from the Drill Hall and I can in all honesty say that as Honorary Colonel I was a little bit more than just a figurehead, acting at times as a commander, training officer and even quartermaster.

I enjoyed it. It was a great privilege to be closely associated with parachute volunteers and to note their enthusiasm, efficiency and high morale. They are very fine soldiers, second to none. I visited them at annual camp all over the place including one in BAOR taking part in an ambitious exercise with Mike Walsh's 3rd Division.

In passing it is worth recording that Mike Walsh on his retirement as a Major General had the distinction of being appointed Chief Scout. In this capacity he did an outstanding job. To my surprise I too was co-opted into the Scout

Movement and became Chairman of the Lincolnshire County Scouts for fourteen years. I knew very little about scouts when I joined but it was a wonderful experience and privilege to work with them. I became convinced that the Scout and Guide Movement is one of the best things left in Britain today.

After eleven years as Honorary Colonel I relinquished the appointment on my 70th birthday. By this time I had completed 50 years' commissioned service in the Army. Admittedly some of it was nominal and unpaid: nevertheless my name did appear in Army officer records for the period January 1935 to April 1985.

4 Para, now under the command of Tony Clark who had previously commanded the Lincoln Company, were kind enough to give me a fine send-off in the form of a Dining-Out Night attended by the Parachute Regimental Colonel Commandant, General Sir Geoffrey Howlett, and Lady Howlett.

Finally, that doctor who had tried to stop me parachuting was probably right. As the years went by I suffered from an increasing amount of pain in my hips. Eventually I had to have one replaced by Sir John Charnley, the founder of hip replacement operations. The other one became equally fractious and had to be dealt with by Group-Captain Murphy, a pupil of Sir John Charnley, at the nearby RAF Hospital at Nocton Hall.

I am deeply grateful to these two surgeons for, so far, the operations have been a great success. Obviously there are aches and pains but in the immortal words of General Sir Frank King, 'If you wake up in the morning and nothing at all aches, then you know you are dead.'

Whereas before the hip replacements I could barely walk the length of one hole of golf, now I can manage two rounds a week.

My golf is not up to the standard of my cricket but, despite two tin hips, I manage to hit the ball reasonably well especially with wooden clubs. But when I reach the green, UGH . . .! It drives me to use a phrase which has been equally applicable to many phases of my military career:

'If only I could putt!'

Appendix A
The Capture of Le Havre
(Chapter 7)

The serious military reader – if there is one – may be interested in how the issue of orders for a big, complex operation was handled at Brigade level and to take a look at a real wartime operation order.

For such an operation as the Capture of Le Havre – "Operation Astonia" – inevitably there is a great deal of bumf. The Divisional Operation Order ran into nearly twenty pages. The Brigade Commander, Henry Wood, and I developed a technique which endeavoured to cut down the paper work and at the same time give the Battalion Commander as much time as possible. The object always in mind was to minimize the burden on the small Battalion staff and to help the soldier as much as possible. After all it was the soldier who in the end had to carry out the Commanders' orders in the teeth of enemy opposition.

Henry would give his outline plan as early as possible and leave me to fill in the details. Then I would issue a warning order or in some cases as for Operation "Astonia" an Operation Instruction. Thus when it came to the Brigade Commander's verbal O Group there was no need to repeat what had been previously made known to all and it could be kept reasonably simple. Maximum use was made of traces to record the detail about objectives, routes and the like. Information about the enemy was issued separately by the Intelligence Officer as it became available.

Paper work had to be produced in the field with what would seem today very primitive equipment and conditions. We were blessed with an excellent Chief Clerk who could take down orders direct on a typewriter and produce them accurately and quickly complete with correct staff duties; no mean feat. He became Editor of "Soldier" magazine.

In spite of these fine sentiments I find to my chagrin that my Brigade Operation Order was a pretty lengthy screed; it now follows in a slightly abridged form.

TOP SECRET
B.L.A.
9 Sep 44

Copy No_______

147 Inf Bde 0.0 No. 18

Ref Map 1:50,000 7 E/4 and 8 E/3

Ref Overprint:– France 1:25.000 LE HAVRE composite Defence Overprint 9

"OPERATION ASTONIA"

INFM

1. Enemy

   As issued separately on Traces, Def overprints and Summaries

2. Own Tps

   (a) See 147 Inf BDE Op Instr No. 11 dated 7 Sep 44

   (b) 56 Inf Bde

   (i) Is making the initial attack with:–

   RIGHT – 2SWB

   LEFT – 2 GLOS

   (ii) 2 ESSEX is to obtain a brhead on feature 535297

   (iii) East Timings –

   H Hr – 1745 hrs (definite)

   1745 hrs – Inf cross SL

   1900 hrs – Leading Inf enter gaps

   2015 hrs – Objective captured up to 31 NORTHING

   2345 hrs – brhead secured by 2 ESSEX

   (c) 152 Inf Bde

   Is attacking on the RIGHT of 49 Div with task of securing a base in the area 510625-510310. Probable H HR 2359hrs D day

   (d) 146 Inf Bde

   (i) Has the following tasks:–

   To simulate an attack during the attack by 56 Bde

   Clear all enemy EAST of R LEZARDE within their bndy

   Br the river, and be prepared to clear the area to the WEST of it, and to pass through into LE HAVRE.

   (ii) Provisional Timing:– 0600hrs D plus 1

   (iii) As an alternative, HALLAMS are being held ready to move via MONTIVILLIERS through 147 Bde to mop up the area centre pt 540280, and subsequently move on to LE HAVRE. LOs are being sent from HALLAMS to 11 RSF and 7 DWR. If this action takes place, a guide from 147 Bde will meet HALLAMS at rd junc 581309.

   (e) RN

   Op is being supported by two monitors of the RN

   (f) RAF

   Timings for Bomber Command tasks are as follows:–

   ALVIS – 1645 – 1745hrs

   BENTLEY – 1845 – 1900hrs

   BUICK – 1900 – 1930hrs

   CADILLAC – a.m D plus 1, to be completed by 0800hrs

3. Additional Tps
   (a) Under comd 147 Inf Bde:–
      219 A Tk Bty RA
      B Coy 2 KENSINGTONS
   (b) In sp 147 Inf Bde:–
      107 RAC
      One Tp C Sqn 22 Dgns (reverting from 56 Bde)
      222 Sqn ARE less one Tp (reverting from 56 Bde)
      One SP Tp 62 A Tk Regt RA
      756 Fd Coy RE
      One pl 240 Fd Coy RE

4. Bndys
   RIGHT Bdny with 51 Br (H) Div:–
      all inc 49 Div track junc 537343 – X rd and track 535339-track junc 531321 – track bend 523314 – all incl 51 Div br 520310 – bend in track 505301 – thence rd to X rds 504291 – X rds 503286 – thence rd to X rds 486283 – X rds 481283 – X rds 477280 – bend in rd 475280

INTENTION

5. 147 Inf Bde Gp will:–
   (a) capture high ground 533296 – 543295 – 544279 – 537280
   (b) Mop up SOUTHERN part of FORET DE MONTGEON and built up area around 530285 – 525296 – 536280 – 513284

METHOD

6. Op will be carried in 4 Phases:–

Preliminary Phase	Clearing route fwd
Phase 'A'	Est firm base area centre pt 522303 Code Word – NORAH
Phase 'B'	est brhead high ground about copse 534293 (NANCY). Code Word – OLGA
Phase 'C'	Capture of high ground between built-up area and R LEZARDE as far South as 544279 Code Word – PAULINE

PRELIMINARY PHASE

7. Tps
   1 LEICESTERS, with in sp:–
      One Pl 756 Fd Coy RE
      One Pl 240 Fd Coy RE

8. Tasks
   (a) Clear slopes of hill from 542320 – 5451309 of enemy
   (b) Open route fwd

9. Timings
   This phase will start on orders from Bde HQ, NOT before 1930hrs D day

PHASE 'A'

10. Tps

1 Leicesters, with under command:–
One Sec 756 Fd Coy RE

and in sp:–
Div Arty, incl One Med Regt
Two Secs 160 Fd Amb

11. Tasks
(a) Clear village 529301
(b) Clear enemy posns on EAST edge of FORET DE MONTGEON 5130
(c) Secure brs at 528305 (URSULA) and 530303 (VIOLET), and report whether blown
(d) Est firm base centre pt 522303

12. Timings

H Hr will be ordered by BDe HQ; NOT before 2359 hrs D day

PHASE 'B'

13. Tps

11 RSF, with under command:–
One Sec 756 Fd Coy RE
One PL B Coy 2 KENSINGTONS

and in sp:–
Div Arty, incl One Med Regt
Two Secs 160 Fd Amb

14. Tasks
(a) To pass between 1 LEICESTERS and 2 ESSEX and clear valley as far SOUTH as rd junc 525296
(b) Est brhead high ground about copse 534293
(c) If enemy resistance is weak, continue to adv SE along high aground as far as possible
(d) In the event of 56 Bde (2 ESSEX) NOT obtaining a brhead area 535297, to carry out this task first, and then continue to do as much of task (a) and (b) above as possible

15. Timings

H Hr will be ordered by Bde HQ; probably NOT before 0200hrs D plus 1

PHASE 'C'

16. Tps

7 DWR, with under command:–
One Sec 756 Fd Coy RE
One Pl B Coy 2 KENSINGTONS

17. Task

To complete capture of high ground as far SOUTH from 536280 – 5442791

18. Timings

H Hr will be ordered by Bde HQ: NOT before 0800hrs D plus 1

19. Res

107 RAC less One Sqn
One Tp 62 (SP) A Tk Regt
756 Fd Coy RE less One Pl
Two Pls B Coy 2 KENSINGTONS
Such flails, Crocodiles, and AVREs as may be available after attack by 56 Bde

20. Exploitation

Any sign of wilting on the part of the enemy will be exploited to the maximum

21-23. Fire sp

details of fire sp by Arty and MMGs

24-26. Routes

details of routes, code words, allocation, traffic control, use of tpt

ADM

27. Med

CCP (187 Fd Amb) – MONTIVILLIERS

28-30. *details of amm res, B Ech, recovery*

31. PW

(a) At H HR, present Div Cage will close, and will open at 643337 under control of 2 KENSINGTONS
(b) On capture of LE HAVRE, a PW Cage will be est in gen area rly sta 5327
(c) Bde PW Collecting Pt – MONTIVILLIERS CATTLE MARKET

32. Remaining adm issued separately

INTERCOMN

33. HQs

details of locations of verious HQs

34. LOs

(a) LO with 152 (H) Bde – Capt Wallace
(b) LO from 22 Dgns, 141 RAC, and 22 Sqn ARE will come to Bde HQ when 56 Bde attack is finished

35. D Day
10 Sept 44

ACK

Major
BM 147 Inf Bde

Time of Signature 2200 hrs
Method of Dispatch – SDR and LO